MASTERING YOUR LIFE

ON THE ENLIGHTENED PATH

SCOTT E. CLARK

Bodhi Publishing Company, LLC
Phoenix, Arizona, USA

Library of Congress Control Number: 2016902686
Tradepaper ISBN: 978-0-9903198-1-8
1st printing, March 2016
Printed in the United States of America

WITH GRATITUDE

I offer appreciation for all of the many teachers that have supported me within this human experience. Each of you has played a role in shaping my present reality and level of consciousness, leading to the message in this book series.

I also express my gratitude to all people who are endeavoring to live enlightened. The world needs your light in whatever unique form or method you have been gifted to provide it.

I forever acknowledge my greatest blessing in this life as the gift of my children, grandchildren, and family. You bring me so much joy, and make it possible for me to continue to heal, grow, and evolve, as I walk this journey of loving service and the sharing of Divine wisdom.

Thank you to Etana Holowinko (www.livesocietyjazz.com) for your talent and inspiration in the design of the cover, and for other technical and artistic contributions. Also, I would like to show appreciation to the great contemporary teachers of higher truth. One who has positively impacted my life with his message and writing is Dr. Wayne W. Dyer. He has recently transitioned from this world, but I thank him for his great contribution of love, light, and higher truth.

TABLE OF CONTENTS

INTRODUCTION

"You are not a human being in search of a spiritual experience. You are a spiritual being immersed in a human experience."

- Pierre Teilhard de Chardin

We all move through our lives wanting to BE better and DO better, in whatever way we have defined this. Maybe we want to be better at our jobs, our relationships, our health, our parenting, or we want greater happiness, with more love, joy, peace, prosperity, and fulfillment in this human experience. In general, we just want a "better life." The good news is that this is available to you.

In truth, you must learn to be the "Master" of your life. Your highest endeavor is Self-Mastery, which is learning to love and honor our unique life path. This ongoing process involves understanding and accepting the gifts and qualities that are special and distinctive to each of us. We have a purpose and a mission to fulfill, that can be defined as our truth. As we move into alignment with this truth, we become authentic, and through the power of our energy we will create the positive qualities we most desire to experience in our life.

Otherwise, the typical way that we have tried to pursue a "better life," is through our ego identification. We are trying to follow the rules and expectations as determined by other people, or society in general. Unfortunately, this has been largely responsible for creating much of our dissatisfaction. We've been taught to search and strive for our desired life according to the approval and perceptions of others. We have sought happiness and fulfillment outside of ourselves.

However, the overriding principle for attaining this better life is to shift our perspective inward. We are to focus on gaining an inner alignment with the higher energy and purpose that come when we are living connected to our authentic life. This is also known as Self-Realization, and is an inner focus that facilitates our shifting toward healing the energy within, rather than determining our wellness from our external circumstances. This transformation requires that we learn a higher wisdom, that we become the master of our life.

We must learn to be more accountable for developing our awareness of exactly how we express our energy, leading to the creation of our outer conditions. For each of us, these expressions take the form of our thoughts, words, feelings, and actions. This is actually energy that in each present moment is creating something in our lives.

What is it that you want to create? Do you want to live your highest truth, and discover your greatest satisfaction, wellness, and growth? How about finding more meaning and fulfillment in service to the world? These are things that you were designed to achieve in this human experience, but you must first connect to your own higher truth.

The purpose of this book series, *On the Enlightened Path*, is to assist you in gaining the insight and wisdom that may support you in shifting from your past limiting beliefs and disempowering perceptions, and connect to your true power and purpose. *Mastering Your Life* is the first book in this series, because it is essential that we recognize our true higher identity, and then create the force of our intention to re-align us onto our true path of enlightenment. This typically requires a powerful inner shifting and awakening to the very truth that we are, in fact, Masters.

This may require learning a new language that offers you greater possibilities and potential. For many this is a new education in empowerment. While learning this wisdom you will be responsible for unlearning and releasing much of the disempowering ego training that is pervasive in the world today. This new information is to be utilized according to your understanding, and desire for healing and growth. You are on your own unique life path, as we all are, and you get to decide what truth best honors your purpose.

The term "Awakening" represents a sudden opening and elevating of our consciousness. This is the initial step in your transformation. You then will be set upon a path that requires your ongoing higher awareness in order to truly create your best life, as you learn to integrate your spirituality into your humanity. This becomes your progression in self-mastery over your unique life path.

Enlightenment is not a destination, it is a process. It is realized in each moment whereby you are connected to your higher truth. And as you are able to shift to this awareness and connection of your spiritual nature, you may embody the qualities of enlightenment. Integrating this energy into your human experiences leads to the fulfillment of your greatest potential. This always benefits each of us individually, and supports our collective humanity.

"Mastery," as a process, is applicable to all people in whatever space or circumstance they find themselves. It offers clarity and purpose to all aspects and activities in your life. It provides understanding and meaning to your past experiences, leading to inner healing and growth. Within your unique life path you are supported and inspired to reach higher and to believe more fully in your own identity, value, and destiny. Regardless of your current place in life, you may apply this wisdom to elevate your awareness to the truth of your being.

The value of enlightened living comes in its practical application into our everyday lives. It is not meant to be something we search for as a profound but all too rare spiritual experience. Nor is it a commitment to the ritualistic practices of ancient commandments. Instead it is intended to be an expression or extension of the spiritual being that is your true

3

and authentic identity. This is the shift that requires the awakening of your consciousness.

Even today, rituals, sacred practices, and faith are extremely important and powerful. However, what is most critical and of greatest benefit to humanity is that these practices lead to love, peace, and unity. We must observe a higher calling which accepts, supports, and serves all people.

Our self-mastery does not come at the expense of others, for we are all masters in our own right. We are evolving and awakening to a more personal connection and commitment to the Divine. Each person on Earth was born with the seeds of enlightenment in them. However, they must be intentionally activated with wisdom and awareness in order for us to begin to shift and evolve our way of being in the world. And this must become a sincere and on-going practice, as each present moment brings a new opportunity to express loving energy, or otherwise fall back into old disempowering habits.

Personal and spiritual growth and healing is not one size fits all, it is to be defined and experienced according to your own higher truth, and there are many paths. My purpose is to support you in honoring your path. Even if you are currently committed to the practice of an established religion you may incorporate this wisdom into your life for a greater integration of your spirituality. My intention is not for you to leave your faith, but to live your faith with the greatest love for yourself and all others. I recommend that you allow yourself to absorb this material by tuning into that which may resonate with you as inner truth. Then utilize this information in a way that best suits the achievement of your own higher goals.

Living your humanity in an awakened state is what you came into this life to do. This higher awareness allows you to know the joy, peace, and love available to all equally. It is not found in the comparison, competition, or expectation of others, but in the inner space that knows your true value. This part always knows that **YOU ARE ENOUGH!**

As we can shift our perception from what we thought of as our reality toward one that reflects our actual truth, we can recognize with gratitude and appreciation the many blessings that currently exist in our lives. Then from this place we are in greater alignment to further attract the opportunities we desire. Now this is true Self-Mastery!

My sincere hope is that these words will somehow resonate as the light of truth that you know deep within. And that with an open mind and heart this truth will move you to explore more fervently the true power you have been designed to express as you create your best life. May you be guided by your own inner light to fulfill your own higher purpose. And through the expression of your light into the world, may you elevate the collective consciousness of all life.

WHAT IS MEANT BY THE TERM ENLIGHTENED?

"Enlightenment is not about becoming divine. Instead it is about becoming fully human...It is the end of ignorance"

- Lama Surya Das

Words can be tricky, in that they can mean different things to different people. We can choose to associate this word "enlightened" with the mystics of past ages who attempted to embody this elusive form of being and state of mind. But if we think of it simply as a far-off unattainable concept, then it really has very little relevance in our lives. Therefore, of what significance is this term to our modern way of thinking and living in the 21st century?

Enlighten means, "to give intellectual or spiritual light," or "to shed light upon." The Buddha reportedly said that "Enlightenment is the end of suffering." What this really means to us today is that we can shine the light of truth and understanding upon the self-imposed obstacles and false perceptions that have caused suffering in the various aspects of our life. Then with a full view of this wisdom we may reveal a new path that leads us to supporting and sustaining a higher quality of life for all. Hence, *The Enlightened Path.*

As we evolve on the level of energy, the highest qualities of life become more accessible. That is the point of evolution. For all of the technological advancements within our human lifestyle, we still retain the essence of our higher nature (Spirit), that when accessed, reflects our highest inner qualities and capabilities. And, it is always important to connect with each

7

other from a loving, caring space, if we are to coexist and flourish.

Enlightenment is an on-going process of inner development that leads us to our greatest meaning and the fulfillment of our Soul's purpose here on Earth. This pertains to us as individuals and as a species. How much better is it to utilize society's modern advancements within a culture that is mutually supportive and invested in the wellbeing of all of the world's citizens?

Our job on the planet at this time is to take sincere steps toward utilizing our higher identity and energetic qualities for the betterment of all life – in other words to **Evolve**. We are gaining the ability to access virtually unlimited amounts of data in the blink of an eye from a myriad of sources at our finger tips. And this speaks to the incredible power of our human instrument – the brain. Yet, are we losing the ability to be fully present, to effectively communicate, and empathize with other people? Of what benefit is it when people are stressed out, while disconnected from their higher energy, and on a pace that is unsustainable. And how do we all benefit while living in a world where people are so consumed and focused on what they can *get* instead of what they can *give*?

Our enlightened path includes intellect and compassion, wisdom and knowledge, heart and mind. The highest energetic quality is love, and through our transformation into more enlightened human beings it is our evolutionary journey to offer and share very practical examples of love in this world. Enlightenment supports us in *giving* this energy to ourselves, as opposed to taking energy from others. This leads to self-mastery, and brings us our greatest reward and achievement.

Enlightenment can and must become integrated by more individuals within our many and varied human experiences. And to this end, it starts with you and me. This is the only thing that can bring about a significant shift in the way we think about ourselves and relate to each other. We can literally create a new reality.

When we can recognize and accept that we are in fact, all spiritual beings having a human experience, we can not only access the higher power within us, but we may identify and treat others with greater love and respect. Regardless of how the appearance of our unique life paths looks amongst all humans, our ultimate journey and origin is the same. We won't always agree with each other's thoughts, words, or actions. Yet, if we can recognize and focus on our commonality we can approach our interactions with greater love, and acceptance of our differences.

As they say, there is no "there" there. In other words, our purpose is not to reach "total enlightenment," somewhere out there in the future. Instead it is a steady application of our higher awareness within each present moment and in all aspects of our human experience.

This is not a "zoned-out," blissful state of consciousness that renders us unable to effectively function in our world. Quite the contrary, it is the highest form of accountability and mindfulness, focusing on the pure love and joy that is available in a mutually supportive presence. In Oneness we are connected with the Divine Presence of Source (God) and with the presence of Divinity within all other beings.

Enlightened living is self-regulated, and self-defined. You have both the freedom and responsibility to develop and experience your own path of healing, growth, and ascension. There is no outer standard, judgment, nor arbitrary scale to conform with. If your intention and practice is to love all others equally, then your path is an enlightened path.

This is a personal journey from where you are in the present, to a state of consciousness that offers more love and light to yourself and all others. There is no ceiling to where you can go, contingent upon your willingness to earnestly and honestly apply yourself. We all start from where we are, and dependent upon the quality of our intentions and practices, versus the challenge of our attachments, we all have the opportunity to transform into a more loving and evolved being. The choice, as free will dictates, is always ours.

MEDITATION PRACTICE:
A TOOL FOR ENLIGHTENED LIVING

"In the attitude of silence the soul finds the path in a clear light, and what is elusive and deceptive resolves itself into crystal clearness. Our life is a long and arduous quest for truth."

- Mahatma Gandhi

A regular meditation practice is a powerful tool for supporting your ongoing self-mastery. It can bring you into direct alignment with your Authentic Self. Something important to understand is that meditation is less about "doing" and more about "being." BE open, BE available to Spirit, BE free from outer and mental distractions, BE the master that prioritizes your life and wellness.

It asks not for exertion or force, but instead for allowance and acceptance. We are required to let go and release the typically frantic energy that finds us in pursuit of some outward goal or random busyness. This instantly creates a challenge for most people, especially those of us raised in the U.S.

A regular meditation practice requires patient and consistent engagement within your own quiet inner space. This is a practice that reinforces that your life is a process that takes place in the present, and that you are more than your thoughts and activities. Your aim is to connect to the energy of your own higher truth; a requirement for self-mastery.

This is often quite subtle to our physical senses, and yet at times, we may experience profound insights. Judge this not on the immediacy of tangible results, but instead, shift your mind to accept that this is a gradual progression that leads to healing, growth, and ascension. It is an activity that generally supports an enlightened life, and is not always an end unto itself.

Meditation has been an established practice for supporting healing and enlightenment for thousands of years. The Bhagavad Gita (which means "Song of the Blessed One") is an epic poem written as early as the fifth century B.C.E., with Lord Krishna offering a teaching to the warrior hero Arjuna about life, deathlessness, nonattachment, the Self, love, spiritual practice, and the inconceivable depths of reality. Using the English translation by Stephen Mitchell, Chapter 6 verses 33-36 (p. 95) reads as follows:

Arjuna said:
You have taught that the essence of meditation is equanimity, Krishna; but since the mind is so restless, how can that be achieved?

The mind is restless, unsteady, turbulent, wild, stubborn; truly, it seems to me as hard to master as the wind.

The Blessed Lord said:
You are right, Arjuna; the mind is restless and hard to master; but by constant practice and detachment it can be mastered in the end.

Meditation is indeed hard for those who lack self-restraint; but if you keep striving earnestly, in the right way, you can reach it.

As this passage relates, meditation, while a key tool for enlightened living, has never been especially easy for mankind. And now, even more than in ancient times, our mind tries to resist surrendering to the quiet power of our higher nature. We have learned to fill our lives with distractions that move us farther away from our truth.

The act of maintaining this practice requires the more subtle, yet powerful, qualities of discipline, self-love, detachment, acceptance, and surrender. Again, these are all worthy qualities to help awaken and shift us to live all of our human experiences in a higher perspective.

While I know meditation to be an indispensable tool for enlightened living, rather than dictate precise methods and techniques, I prefer to allow each individual to find their own inner patterns and process. However, I believe that it is important to just jump in and get started without feeling like you need to be an expert first. To this end, I have detailed some basic information later in this chapter that you may find helpful. If after some personal experience you wish to research and practice various other specific methods, by all means do so.

If you are already engaged in a meaningful meditation practice, please continue what you are doing. Accordingly, you may skip the remainder of this section if you wish. I am happy to give you my views on what seems to work for me, but ultimately it must fit your needs in order to be taken seriously and practiced regularly. You already know the tremendous value and may be comfortable with your own techniques. This chapter was written primarily for those with little or no experience in such things.

I would be hard pressed to find anyone who has not heard of meditation, especially in this day and age. However, maybe you are someone who has never really considered this practice for yourself. Everything we do, when we are developing ourselves with the idea of getting better or more proficient, takes practice. While not everything takes the same amount of practice, the more importance we place on our goals, the more willing we are to put in the work.

In this sense, a regular meditation practice is like any other learned skill (like consistently and accurately hitting a golf ball for example). Of course, you would only put in the practice to master this skill if it were of a sufficient priority for you do this. Equally true is that we don't just wake up one day and suddenly play golf ball like a pro, nor do we instantly become an expert in meditation. Well, the good news is that meditation is easier and cheaper to master than golf, or whatever technical skill was likely required to master your job. But it does take persistent practice.

The reward for engaging in this regular practice is that you will become more in tune with your spiritual nature, your inner peace, your present-moment energy, and the higher guidance that can support you in any area of life. Seems like a very worthwhile goal and a pretty good payoff for a few quiet, inwardly-focused moments a day.

"All of man's difficulties are caused by his inability to sit, quietly, in a room by himself."

- Blaise Pascal

As with many things in life, your intentions are very powerful. If you can look at this tool with a mind that is free from prejudice, and a heart filled with the desire to practice regularly for the potential benefit that may be realized, you will surely achieve more than you thought was possible. The goal, as with most healthy practices, is to develop this as a daily habit. In other words, schedule a time and make it automatic; in this way the mind has little chance of talking you out of it before it becomes ingrained and established.

Of course, as most of our obstacles are self-made, the mind can sabotage this activity quickly if you're not careful. People who have not given this a fair try may think, "I can't just sit there doing nothing," or "That is weird, what would people think if they knew?" Or "I can't slow down my thoughts, my mind just races," or "It is uncomfortable for me to sit in that position." Pretty standard excuses for people who either do not understand the benefit or the process/techniques of meditation.

Let me address these excuses. "I can't just sit there doing nothing" may likely be the same person whose mind won't slow down. It is true that people have different issues with attention, and A.D.D. (attention deficit disorder) seems to be rampant in our society. This is all the more reason to teach meditation to children and adults. I am certainly not diagnosing or prescribing treatment for any illnesses. However, in addition to the appropriate medical advice, if you have great difficulty focusing and clearing your mind, then increased patience and persistence may be required.

When one's lifestyle is overly frantic and physically/mentally active, you are effectively eliminating or diminishing your opportunities to experience your powerful inner space. This is the connection to your higher awareness and consciousness. Therefore, this is the person who may realize the greatest shift and growth from a meditation practice.

I have heard it said that if you cannot find the time to meditate once a day, you are a person who should be meditating twice a day. In reality you have all of the hours of the day to be as physically active as you want, you have plenty of time for the "doing" that you think is so significant. And the real truth of life is that we will always make time for the things we deem most vital.

For most people the problem is not that they cannot sit still and find some space between thoughts, the problem is that their mind is relatively untrained and undisciplined. When this is the case, not being able to meditate is likely the least of your problems. The lack of an ability to focus our minds will affect us in all areas of life, and render us unreliable to ourselves and others.

Embarking on a meditation practice helps to solve many of the challenges we create for ourselves. Finding the space of self-realization in your meditation is creating time for "being." This not only relates to connecting with your Authentic Self, but it is also space for being something more than your thoughts, actions, interactions, and human distractions. For you this might lead to more moments throughout your hectic day to be reminded of this space that is always available with your awareness. This may provide added clarity and peace, and likely improve your expressions of energy and experiences with others.

As for "that is weird...," meditation is something you do for yourself. It is not a showy display designed to impress anyone, nor is it an activity that needs to be approved of by others. It is a solemn practice designed for personal growth and spiritual connection. For those who do not believe in anything spiritual, think of it as a few moments to find peace within yourself, apart from the stress and noise of the world. With respect to its being physically uncomfortable, you do not have to sit cross legged on a cushion, you can just as effectively meditate sitting in a chair.

In addition to providing a direct connection to your spiritual essence, meditation is becoming universally recognized as a valuable technique and daily practice to help alleviate stress and its effects on the health of the body. *Time Magazine* reported this in an article from November 14, 2012, called, "Strongest study yet shows meditation can lower risk of heart attack and stroke." This article refers to a scientific study in the American Heart Association journal which provided the following conclusion:

"A selected mind-body intervention, the TM (Transcendental Meditation) program, significantly reduced risk of mortality, myocardial infarction, and stroke in coronary heart disease patients. These changes were associated with lower blood pressure and psychosocial stress factors. Therefore, this practice may be clinically useful in the secondary prevention of cardiovascular disease."

Stress is really a disconnection from our Authentic Self (Spirit). We have moved away from our inner peace in order to attach to an outside disturbance or imbalance. Engaging in a meditation practice reconnects us to our true identity, the aspect of ourselves that is more powerful than the problems we perceive to be our reality. Within our truth we are not the problem, situation, or event that triggered the stress attack. Therefore, we can shift our awareness to the more loving space of our Being. We can remember to just breathe. And then from this place be more empowered to take the best and most appropriate steps toward resolving our human issues.

So How Do I Begin?

It is my hope that you are now willing to commit to a personal meditation practice for the sake of elevating your wellness and consciousness. Here are some of the steps that may be taken in order to get started:

- **Find your outer space** – I suggest that you find or create a space or setting that is relatively quiet and peaceful. To the extent you can, you want to avoid external distractions. There will be enough to contend with from your own mind. You can either meditate indoors or outdoors, as long as it is comfortable and peaceful.

- **Make it Sacred** – Use your heartfelt intentions to make this a sincere practice. Wherever you define to be your physical space, include in proximity things that inspire you. For instance I meditate facing a table which holds candles, incense, small statues or pictures of various enlightened Masters, and other miscellaneous symbolic items.

This is the space in my home that I use exclusively for my meditation. You just need sufficient space, not an entire room. But make this special and sacred for you, and incorporate anything that might be particularly inspiring or helpful to honor your Authentic Self.

I do not meditate with music, however, if you wish to play appropriate music at a low volume in the background, you can see if this helps you to relax your mind. Still others may want to follow an audio "guided meditation," and would therefore need access to the appropriate equipment or device.

    - Please be seated – I suggest that for reasons of comfort and alertness you practice your meditation in a seated position. As you become more adept with mindfulness you can effectively meditate while walking or performing other activities. However, while being more mindful in all we do is our goal, it is preferred to just focus on this one task at a time.

    Lying in a prone position is fine for prayers or affirmations just prior to falling asleep or after waking up, but generally less effective for meditation. If this is your only option, then of course do your best from this position. You can sit cross-legged on a blanket or cushion (as I do), or you can sit in a chair with your feet flat on the ground. Either way, your spine should be straight and your head level with eyes closed.

    - What about timing? – I suggest you start out meditating once a day, for 15 - 20 minutes. As you develop your practice you may eventually want to increase your time and/or add a second daily meditation. Depending upon your daily schedule, personal habits, and body clock, you can decide what time of day works best for you.

    However, I do not recommend meditating at the end of the evening just prior to going to sleep, as you will be more likely to doze off and lose the alert but calm focus you need. Remember the initial goal is to make this practice yours and to be consistent. If I tell you when to practice, because it is what works for me, then this would not honor your truth.

    You are creating a positive, healthy practice as part of your lifestyle, and it helps to form a pattern in your mind as to your designated time slot. If you are able to meditate in the morning before you start your workday, this often works best for many people. As life moves around you and occasionally disrupts this time, don't worry, be flexible. All is happening now in perfect order; allow what is, but reconnect to your commitment as quickly as you can.

- **What is my motivation?** – Make the effort to embrace gratitude, surrender, and enthusiasm. Since this is a regular daily practice, you will sometimes engage in meditation with energy that is peaceful and joyful, while at other times you will feel anxious, stressed, or angry. Life is bringing your awareness to all of the various energies that exist, therefore, we meditate from where we are in that moment.

That said, this is also a good time to do your best to release your attachment to whatever your present energy happens to be. You are not resisting or denying it, you are simply setting it aside with a shift in awareness and an intention to release its power over you. You are simply using these next few moments to honor yourself and remember your truth.

The way you make this shift is to bring in the energy of gratitude and surrender. Even when negatively charged, you can be grateful for this opportunity to be free for a few minutes as you connect to your Higher Self. Disengage or detach from the perceptions that are creating the negative energy around a particular circumstance or experience. Be reminded that your external concerns represent the temporary struggle of false perception (ego) that is currently a part of your path. Find appreciation for this higher understanding.

The other key quality that is useful for shifting away from distracting energy in your meditation is surrender. This is the equivalent of moving from effort and force to allowance and calmness. Your ego wants to control all situations and people, which have likely caused whatever problem you are dealing with. In order to release this energy we must allow our true higher nature to become our focus over our ego. This is the aim in quieting the mind, not always an easy thing to do when we are disturbed.

Remember, our Spirit is always present, but it will not overtake our free will. And our ego is like a child who constantly demands our attention. We must release our ego for the moments of this practice in order to surrender to the subtle, yet powerful voice within us. Sometimes it is about being more aware of the space between our thoughts, and then returning to this space as often as necessary.

When we come to our meditation from a place of peace and joy, it will of course be easier to feel gratitude because our ego is fairly self-satisfied in this moment. However, we still must surrender our ego energy in order to more fully connect to our Authentic Self, which is beyond the duality of good or bad perceptions.

Typically, the energy that is distracting us is based on some judgement about the past or future, and we are now becoming ever so present. Our focus is far less on releasing negativity, and more about shifting toward gratitude and surrender. Our best focus is always on the positive energy we desire to create, and not the fearful energy we are overcoming.

Adding the energy of enthusiasm brings a deeper Divine quality to our enlightened practice. This word comes from the original Greek to mean: *To be inspired from God.* This is a powerful quality for creating or manifesting higher desires in your life.

- What do I do now? – Ok, you are seated in your sacred outer space, and you have shifted to the proper motivation for your practice, what's next? Of course, it depends on whom you talk to. I usually start by extending my motivation of gratitude to include prayers (thought expressions) of thanks and appreciation to Divine Source. I also include the Angels and Spirit Guides who are offering their guidance, support, and protection at this time. I give thanks for this day of life, regardless of what I perceive in my human experience. I know that each present moment's focus on higher possibilities has the power to shift my outer experiences.

I take the initial first few minutes to ask and give thanks for the guidance that I am seeking in order to fulfill my higher purpose. This could be in general or for certain projects (for example my writing and teaching). If I am feeling that my energy is disturbed by some particular event, person, or experience, I will ask to see clearly the truth that I am being taught for purposes of deeper healing and growth. **I am asking for enlightenment.**

Next I will try to clear my thoughts and settle the wandering of my mind. I may focus on my breath in and out for a period of time until things settle. The one physical function that is life sustaining, in which we may be aware of in the present moment, is our breath. There are many different breathing techniques that may be used in meditation. Other types of meditation involve a single-pointed mental focus on a specific object. If you are interested, you may study these techniques further on your own.

For now, simply noticing your breathing takes your focus away from your thoughts and that endless mental to-do list. You will only be able to follow your breath for so long before, hopefully, you will open to your inner awareness which functions independently from your conscious thoughts. If you lose this space due to new thoughts running through your head, simply acknowledge the thought without judgment and return to your breathing.

Another thing that you can add to your meditation practice, if you wish, is to spend a few moments with positive affirmations. This is not meant to be a substitute for clearing your mind, just something you may want to add at the beginning or end. With this we repeat positive statements (non-verbally) in our mind for the purpose of helping us to continue shifting the way in which we have often "defined" ourselves while in our weakened ego perceptions.

You can refer to your Divine qualities like: I am enlightened (peaceful, joyful, loving, abundant, healthy, etc.). Or to any of your roles such as: I am a successful author (teacher, accountant, parent, etc.). Or the one that I love the best is simply: "How may I serve?" When understood beyond the level of ego, this goes right to the heart of gratitude, surrender, and enthusiasm. Of course you are welcome to do affirmations anytime during the day that they come into your mind.

- What am I supposed to get from meditation? - The primary objective is to experience a release of your endless thoughts and total identification with your mind and external stimulation; during this period and beyond. Of course, our ego always wants to know, "what's in it for me?"

Some of the benefits of meditation will be quite subtle or not perceived at all. Remember that this process is more directly applicable to inner development - leading to outer achievement. Each practice (or step) adds something whether or not it is detectible to us.

During this brief time of your meditation you may or may not have become aware of a connection to your Authentic Self (Spirit). For some people it will take a longer amount of experience before they can begin to relax their mind, release their physical senses, and not feel self-conscious. Stay with your commitment to yourself, and remind your ego often that this is not a competition - and stop judging!

Over time you will begin to feel more relaxed and perhaps lighter as the practice becomes more natural and part of your lifestyle. On occasion you may become aware of a connection to Spirit by receiving specific insights, wisdom, or clarity that you may understand as coming from somewhere other than your own mind. This will likely feel very profound and supportive to you in some way.

When this happens, some people tend to get visions that are showing them some picture or message. Other people (like me) are more auditory and may be inclined to hear words as a message. In any case, you will recognize this as something outside of your normal ego thought potential, and it will feel like a powerful truth for you. Much like the dream state, this is a place where Spirit can make contact with us more easily.

If you are doing something creative or are specifically inspired and reliant upon this higher wisdom, this may happen more frequently. I meditate before I write, and sometimes, I start receiving certain words or phrases that I am supposed to include in my writing. I will jot this down on a note pad. If it continues I will just get up and go to the computer to start my writing session.

The point is that you are creating a space for personal connection to your Divine Self. It always knows what you need for support, healing, and growth. This can be a gentle way for you to receive what you need without necessitating an outer experience, where ego often blocks or dilutes the message. By the way, I advise keeping pen and paper handy just in case something profound comes through for you, as you may not remember it later.

You may not always be aware of receiving higher communications, most people are not. Yet your guides are trying to communicate with you. On the level of energy, they are doing this from such a high frequency that we often are unable to receive it. Even so, we are still benefiting from our meditation practice.

We are breathing more calmly, lowering our heart rate, and creating a more peaceful feeling about our human life. We are intentionally creating the space to recognize and honor our Authentic Self. And establishing this practice as a regular part of our daily lifestyle will naturally lead us to be more mindful of our thoughts, feelings, words, and actions throughout our other activities. This is a big part of mastering your life.

Once you begin to receive the benefit of true wellness from healthier habits, you no longer need to sabotage your life.

This is the truth of spiritual practice and enlightened living. It is an elevated state of awareness (or consciousness) that is a path for wellness and true success. I hope that you will endeavor and persist with a daily meditation practice in support of the powerful awakening you are now creating in your life.

PART I:

REALIZING YOUR AUTHENTIC SELF

"Virtually every spiritual tradition teaches that your higher self is the presence of God within you."

- Dr. Wayne W. Dyer

PART I: Prologue

The first step to Mastering Your Life is to understand that you ARE a Master. Whether or not you have been aware of this, you have a higher identity. I am calling this your "Authentic Self." Within the wisdom of this teaching, there are two main ways to think of this term. One, your Authentic Self represents your Divinity, often called Spirit or Soul. You have been brought into form as an individuation of the Universal or Divine Energy that permeates all life. It is this higher aspect of you that exists before, during, and beyond this human experience.

And two, your Authentic Self represents the truth of the life you are to live as human. You chose to come here to honor and fulfill your unique path and purpose. Your individual gifts, qualities, passions, physicality, personality, and initial circumstances were specifically designed for this journey. Before our worldly education pulls us into a false identification with ego, we were well aware of our higher path.

We are spiritual beings having this unique human experience. Your Authentic Self knows who you are, why you are here, and the true value of this opportunity. Ultimately, you have chosen Earth school as a part of your Soul's journey in healing, growth, and ascension.

In "Realizing" your Authentic Self, you are recognizing and accepting this identity and causing it to become real, as the foundation of your truth. Another term for this is Self-Realization. From this perspective we may form the basis of creating and living the Divine qualities that we most desire, within our humanity. This is an awakening that shifts you onto a more enlightened path.

PART I: Energetic Quality or Tool

The Divine energetic tool to be used in Realizing your Authentic Self is *ACCEPTANCE*. While functioning in this life from the perspective of free will, our ego strives to gain what it wants through effort, struggle, control, and comparison. It tells us that we must "become" something extraordinary in order to be valued and worthy. Of course, this is a false identity that leaves us always wanting more, never satisfied with the reality we are creating.

The fact is, we are already empowered with all of the energetic inner qualities we desire. In place of striving to be something we are not, the tool that supports us most is *acceptance*. We don't have to labor to be our Divine Authentic Self, nor do we need to be ordained by anyone else. It is only for us to accept that which we already are. And then we are to integrate this true higher identity into our humanity. Once we realize this as our truth, even in the light of our human limitations, we may begin to shift our perspective of what is possible and flow from this higher energy source.

The Divine energy of Acceptance will be quite challenging to our ego way of life, as its opposite quality of *RESISTANCE* will attack often. Acceptance of our spiritual truth goes against the preponderance of worldly training and conditioning, which has controlled our minds. Therefore, resistance becomes our inner voice of fear that doubts and challenges the existence of any such higher identity. When living more enlightened, your awareness will shine the light of truth upon the resistance that you will recognize within yourself from time to time.

29

CHAPTER 1

The Truth of Who You Really Are

*"Every man is a divinity in disguise,
a god playing the fool."*

- Ralph Waldo Emerson

Everything that you have come to experience with your physical senses has been defined by you as your identity. This is natural and reasonable since you continually feel the effects of this life upon and within your body or mind. You have a name, a number, a unique DNA makeup that defines your physical characteristics, and you have your own brand of worldly education and training. If your mind is disturbed or your body feels discomfort, you will easily identify with these conditions.

All of this is certainly accurate for each of us. But is that all there is to us in this life? As you know, I am introducing you to another even more powerful and real aspect of yourself. Yet, for us as humans, this may only have relevance in so much as it beneficially impacts our humanity. After all, we have to be able to stay alive, take care of ourselves, interact with others, and pay the bills.

You are a spiritual being having a human experience. Brace yourself, as I am going to reinforce this message often. The "beingness" part of you is your Authentic Self. This is synonymous with your Higher Self or Spiritual Self. If you were merely a human being who had occasional spiritual experiences, then your primary identity would be human. Yet, this is not the case, as your Authentic Self is the identity that comprises your ongoing existence.

How is it that we can realize our Authentic Self while living our humanity? It is my intention throughout this book to offer the practical guidance and wisdom to help you connect to this part of yourself that transcends your exclusive identity with your physical senses. And I hope that by the end you will have a better understanding of your higher truth and purpose for integrating your spirituality into your humanity.

Since we are spiritual beings, we exist on a level beyond this human experience. We exist before, during, and after it. Our energetic reality is Divine Consciousness. And this signifies a Spirit or Soul (I will be using these two terms interchangeably) journey that in some way is our individuation of Divine Source. This may sound strange, or be new information, or it may be a reminder of what you already know to be true. In any case, I hope that you will stay with me to learn more of this higher education.

We do not lose our humanity by identifying with our spirituality. Since it is our higher truth and the aspect of us that chose this human experience and all of the associated details, it is our highest source of support. Conversely, when we overly (or exclusively) identify with our humanity, we will ignore or refute our Authentic Self.

Let me explain. Our humanity consists largely of the things we were born with, including the ways in which we develop based upon our initial circumstances. We identify with these qualities and characteristics. We actually define ourselves by them. When these things lead to societal approval we think we have achieved something great, we are a success. And when our qualities are considered undesirable by others, then we think we are a failure.

In either case, we are each making choices and experiencing our life within a set of parameters and factors that are separate and unique to each person. Is anyone truly accurate in saying they achieved success while someone else is relegated to failure status? This is delusion, and not truth.

Different circumstances, as judged by worldly standards and definitions, favor some outcomes over others. And this all takes place within our lower ego-nature.

If we are a success, we will try to hold on to these accolades and human rewards, and we may prop ourselves up as better than some others. But life changes and moves forward. We grow older, and we may struggle with maintaining health, wealth, power, or prestige. Now maybe we become unsatisfied with our life because we no longer meet the world's definitions of successful. Suddenly we are judged as failures or have-nots.

If we inherited less-desirable conditions, we have a couple choices. One, we can struggle and strive to change our circumstances in some way in order to be recognized by other people as successful. Or two, we can continue to feel like we failed in life, and maybe even see our future as hopeless. In this case the manner in which we judge our own life is dependent upon other people and outer conditions. And we may even become dependent upon other people merely for our survival.

We have been trained to be a slave to our human conditioning. Our identity as "only human" is based in the delusion of fear and limitation. When we take on this human body we are controlled by ego. It is critical to ego that it survives, because it only exists as long as you are in bodily form. It is also primarily concerned about your life conditions with respect to comfort, safety, and approval.

We live within this human identity, as does everyone else, and are all running around trying to make sure that we are taken care of. Success and failure becomes a comparative and relative distinction. This is all ego-based delusion, which can only function within the energy of fear. Of itself, it does not have the capacity to support the energies of love, peace, joy, and wellness

The shift that is required is to become the Master of your Self. Your higher truth offers the potential for a very different reality. You first existed on the level of energy that I will call Spirit. For whatever the process that Divinity requires, you called into existence your human life, for the purposes of spiritual healing, service, and evolution. This includes the design of a life path that serves the Soul. Serving your Soul's purpose is a function of Divine loving energy, and supporting ourselves in this way serves all other Soul journeys as well.

Additionally, as part of your designed path you chose the key humans/Souls that will support you in this process, including your family and others. This is called your Soul Group. You chose your physical characteristics, birth time and place, personality, race, gender, culture, initial socio-economic conditions, etc.

The mere fact that you are here is evidence that you have your own special and unique purpose. You are equally valuable and worthy as anyone else who has chosen a human experience. You simply designed the path and conditions that best serve your Soul's purposes. We are all successes, no one is a failure. We all have the same opportunity to fulfill and achieve our purpose. Yet it will look differently for each of us.

When we simply judge the outer appearance according to our ego standards, we completely miss our truth. And through fear we disempower ourselves and others. Therefore, it becomes essential to awaken from this ego delusion and connect our awareness to identify with our Authentic Self.

You may notice within yourself or others that at times you are loving, peaceful, compassionate, etc., without knowing or identifying with this terminology or spiritual identity. We are Divine whether we know it or not, and this part of us will shine through from time to time. Yet, it is largely blocked when we are attached to our ego identity. However, the wisdom of shifting your identity to this higher aspect will guide you toward intentionally creating the Divine qualities within your human experience more naturally and often.

This signifies the difference between the "enlightened path" versus the typical path of ego. It identifies where we are placing our energy, and the overriding quality of that energy. Are we seeking to offer our highest truth and light into the world for the benefit of all? Are we accepting all other people as living their own Divine Soul/human journey, regardless of their level of consciousness? Or are we primarily focused on having our needs and desires met without any real consideration of other people? You are here to offer your love and light, therefore, you must awaken to realize your true Higher Self.

CHAPTER 2

What is Your View of Reality?

"You move totally away from reality when you believe that there is a legitimate reason to suffer."

- Byron Katie

The pervasive identity that accompanies us as we take on a physical form in this material world is ego. Evan while our non-physical nature remains Spirit, we learn to prioritize our ego existence for the sake of survival. However, the more encompassing view is that when we only recognize our identity as ego, we will perceive all that exists within our field of perception as somehow impacting and defining us. This is the quality that leads humankind to separateness as opposed to unity.

This view of ourselves as the central player in all that exists will define our "reality." In truth it is simply our view of how things affect and impact our desire for comfort, recognition, and security. In and of itself, this is not all bad. Our highest path does not involve neglecting or forsaking our physical/emotional needs. Of course, we must survive in order to fulfill any higher Soul purpose. And while we are here, it is certainly not our intention to struggle and suffer. Yet, this is typically what we do when overly attached to ego.

The problem with the viewpoint from ego, which controls and dominates our life, is that it is based in the energy of fear. This is then fortified and encouraged in nearly all of our worldly training from the time we are born. We learn to think or say, "My way or beliefs are true, and yours are false. I am right and you are wrong. My needs must be met above yours, thus it is okay when I take from you. Accumulating wealth, power, and status is my primary purpose, and it matters not what I have to do to others to attain it."

It may be startling to consider this stark truth of our general egocentric beliefs and behaviors. Yet, can you deny that this is the energy that has created the world we now live in. On a personal level this energy is unsatisfying and unfulfilling, even for those with the rewards society deems the pinnacle of success. And for those "less fortunate," in the delusion of ego, life is intolerable, dangerous, and possibly even hopeless. You may notice that nearly everyone is feeling fearful and disempowered, either trying to keep what they have, or get what they want.

You may ask, well, the "real world" is setup this way, what am I supposed to do about it?" I guess that is the important question. Are you to fix or change it? Are you to accept it and make the best of it? Or are you going to transform and transcend your reality?

Firstly, you can't fix or change other people. Everyone is on their own unique path of purpose and consciousness. So your real choice becomes, do I remain in my ego identity and make the best of a broken system, or do I begin to elevate how I choose to identify myself and learn to experience a higher reality within this world as it exists.

Obviously, the choice for which I am advocating is awakening to your true identity and then creating a new reality whereby you are the master of your life. This will take you upon a more enlightened path. We awaken when we shift our perspective of truth, and live our human life from our greater identity.

I have discussed previously that you are simultaneously Spirit and human; remember, "A spiritual being having a human experience." However, our egoic view most often minimizes or eliminates the Spirit part. Therefore, it is likely that you have been overly consumed with the human aspect, and barely, if at all, aware of your own Spirit.

Due to our need for awakening, most of us have allowed a slumber-like fog, encouraged by the collective unconscious world around us, to create a barrier which blocks our higher awareness. Whether through ignorance or complacency we have primarily lived our lives unaware of our true power and purpose. In order to live enlightened, it is not that we need to be reborn into a new creation. Instead we must accept and become more of what we truly are – Divine.

Our ego perception has permeated all aspects of our human involvement. It infects our beliefs, communications, interactions, and behaviors. It resides in our homes, schools, governments, and religions. Not only has our view of reality been limited, it is literally destructive and dangerous. It is a path consumed in darkness.

We all reside in some level of higher consciousness (connection to Spirit). No one is completely consciousness or unconscious 100% of the time. For purposes of illustration, think of consciousness as light and unconsciousness as darkness.

Imagine your human life as a path. The more you are surrounded by darkness, the less your visibility will be and the more limited your view of the space or qualities around you. It may even be so dark that you only notice yourself. This is the reality that we all have experienced while controlled by ego. We endure our human challenges as we are stumbling down a dark path. We are not evil; we simply lack awareness of our truth.

It is a fearful perception of reality, fraught with the mental images of danger from unseen monsters. Both within our mind and from outside sources we are told that there are enemies out there, and we believe it because we are lost in our fear without the awareness to see truth. Or maybe we are taught that there is a limited supply of everything, therefore we better gather and hoard all we can, before someone else gets ours. This is how we justify our ego behavior, and create suffering.

However, as you add light to your path, you are able to expand your view, and encompass a greater connection with all that is around you. This light is the truth of your Being; it is your Authentic Self. Your awareness has been elevated above the fear that darkness encouraged. You have more choices leading to the recognition of beliefs and practices that support you in being accountable for your own well-being. You may now even see beyond your own self-interests, and discover ways to add light onto the path of others. Enlightenment is about adding a little more light in each present moment.

Best of all, since the source of light is within you, you are not dependent upon others. Consequently, only you can diminish your own light. No one else can make your path dark. Notice that enlightenment requires a tremendous amount of accountability. I hope that you can see that this is a reality that supports you in living a more satisfying, meaningful, and fulfilling life. This enlightened path becomes a reality when you are willing to be the master of your own life.

CHAPTER 3
A Higher Definition of Success

"Try not to become a man of success.
Rather become a man of value."

- Albert Einstein

Certainly, all of the experiences, events, and circumstances in your life will continue to need your active attention as long as you are human. Spirituality does not minimize this. However, you may now realize all of these human endeavors in relation to your understanding of your higher value and potential. True success is self-determinant. It is to be defined by you according to your individual gifts, qualities, passions, interests, and purpose.

Once you stop defining your success by external ego-based standards, no one can rightfully tell you what success should look like for you. For this would only serve to limit you or direct you away from your true path. You have the freedom to define this in ways that are more attainable and supportive to your views of a balanced healthy life.

In truth, what becomes most valuable (successful) is the way you live your life - your habits, practices, intentions, and contributions. Are you experiencing peace, joy, and fulfillment? Then you are successful regardless of what others think, or no matter your income, title, or possessions. Are you surrounding your path with light, and serving the wellness in others in some way? That sounds like success to me, whether your service offers unconditional benefit to one person or to millions.

Success comes from realizing your Authentic Self and living in alignment with the special unique qualities, gifts, and purpose that you are here to express. You have a specific, yet unknown, amount of time within your human experience. To express your love within the fulfillment of your higher purpose during this relatively short span is the most meaningful achievement we can attain. Yet, only you can know your heart and truth.

Defining success as an entitlement to the praise and adoration of others, simply because your life path includes physical prowess or beauty, relative wealth, or a high intellectual aptitude, is really no great achievement at all. I am not telling you that money, physical beauty, nice homes and cars, vacations, or other luxuries are bad. There is nothing within spiritual law that demonstrates that material prosperity and conscious living are mutually exclusive. We have each designed our own unique life path and purpose prior to incarnation, in order to serve our spiritual wellness in some capacity.

While not a spiritual achievement or necessity, some Souls have designed a life path that includes material affluence, or some physical advantage. The problem exists when one resides in a relatively unconscious ego state while realizing these worldly benefits. In this case, as is true for anyone who is disconnected from Spirit, they may be functioning within the control of fear. This fear may lead them to harm or disempower other people in some way. Or they may be insensitive and unaware of any higher purpose or value for having such gifts. Ego tells them that they "earned" this advantage, and if others had worked as hard or as smart as they did, maybe they would have more riches. No one can maintain a connection to their higher truth, within this attitude or perception.

In spite of their prosperity, this is a dark path with little awareness of truth. They are claiming their rewards in this ego world. Yet, they likely are missing their opportunity for greater ascension on a spiritual level.

This may not really concern them now, because they think they are "winning" this game. However, our healing, growth, and evolution is determined in how we live and what we do with our gifts. Did we express loving energy into the world, or fearful energy? Did we add to the light or the darkness?

The primary reason for writing this chapter is to let everyone know that they have within them the possibility of great success according to a higher definition. It is not determined by where and how you grew up, or your level of education or wealth. These are all human qualities that may factor into your life path and the gifts you are here to offer. Yet, within any path of human experience there is opportunity to express your Divine qualities for the betterment of your life and in service to others.

When you live in a manner that is connected to your Authentic Self, you will function within a higher capacity, and express your loving energy. Your job and income may be determined based upon your education, skills, experience, and opportunity within this world. Yet your value may be realized and expressed in your contributions within whatever work is best for you. As the world is presently made up of some 7.2 billion human Souls, there is virtually unlimited need for services which may be a source of fulfillment to you, and provide assistance to someone else.

We only feel worthless, unappreciated, and undesirable when we try to live someone else's life or dream, or when we judge our value by the ego world's standards. You have designed your life to fulfill your unique purpose. Therefore, you may rightfully feel successful, i.e. loved, peaceful, joyful, abundant, fulfilled, and empowered, when you are living your truth.

Awaken to honor your path. Let other people live their path. Be motivated by your opportunities to contribute your best gifts and energy into the world. Endeavor to build upon these gifts by accessing your higher guidance, and taking regular steps toward expanding your capabilities. Be fully accountable for your thoughts, words, and actions, knowing that this energy will manifest into your experiences. Do not expect other people to do your work. As they say, "no one else can do your push-ups." On the enlightened path you utilize both your spirituality and your humanity to create your best reality and definition of success.

CHAPTER 4
Shifting Your Identity

"Spirit is the essence of consciousness, the energy of the Universe that creates all things. Each of us is a part of that spirit – a Divine entity. So the spirit is the higher self, the eternal being that lives within us."

- Shakti Gawain

Some people may consider themselves spiritual or religious, while others claim no such belief or affiliation. While I use a certain language and terminology to communicate my message, the truth is not in the labels or classifications. *Your Authentic Self is something that exists whether or not you call it by that name, or even if you refute such a higher power or distinction.*

It is much more about the intentions with which we live our lives. Here are some questions to ponder. What are your priorities? How and when do you value and accept yourself? How and when do you value and accept ALL other people? Are you living your truth, or someone else's? Are you grateful for your life and all of your experiences, or just the ones that "feel" good? Are you finding ways to offer loving service in contribution to the wellness of other people and the planet?

The answers to these questions reveal your level of consciousness (connection to Spirit). This is not to judge anyone as good or bad, it is a reminder that in this life we have the capabilities to evolve to do and be more. Based upon your answers, you may be living connected to your higher truth, or otherwise overly controlled in some way by ego/fear.

The concept of living more consciously or enlightened pertains to the time you spend connected to the energy of love. Love is the essence of Spirit. Even if you say, "I don't believe in any of that spiritual stuff." Your Spirit is not waiting for you to "believe" in a certain terminology or teaching. It does not need your acknowledgment or approval. Universal Law exists – always. The more you express loving energy the more often you will create loving human conditions. And the more you attach to fear-based energy the more you will live within experiences fraught with fear and suffering.

You may go to church every Sunday or read every spiritual book. And yet, you may live in a manner that is controlled by ego and fear, and is decidedly void of loving expression. For it is not enough to follow rituals, study loving philosophy, or support only those close or similar to us. You must shift your identification and awaken to an elevated level of consciousness. This is a key component to the self-mastery of which I teach.

When expressing fear, judgment, hate, discrimination, insecurity, or lies about any other person or group, you are disconnected from your Spirit. As opposed to calling this evil, or some other negative label, I am saying that this is unconsciousness – a display of unloving energy. You do not have to identify or classify yourself with any particular group or teaching to be loving and conscious. Instead, you must honor your own inner Divinity leading to more loving expressions.

Choosing to connect to your Authentic Self or to ego-control reveals your relative state of consciousness in a particular present moment. We were all raised in ego/fear. This is our human nature. No one is completely free from this delusion that diminishes our truth. Yet, we were also all born with free will and with a higher identity. Through acceptance, we engage the wisdom and power of this potential. And then, with great intention we endeavor to live enlightened, shifting our primary identification, and therefore, our way of living in this world.

It is a matter of prioritizing your inner healing, growth, and evolution, over the delusions and distractions that have previously seduced you. You must shift your focus inward, and examine yourself for the purposes of identifying (remembering) your truth. This includes realizing your gifts, skills, interests, and passions.

You are to view your life from a higher perspective, whereby you will notice the placement and integrity of your energy. You may revise your goals to focus on your inner as well as outer wellness. You can now develop and practice healthy habits to replace the old disempowering ones. You will create a new view of your true value. Now you may find gratitude and appreciation for all that exists. And you will learn to claim your power in the present moment.

You are connecting with your higher identity, and creating a new reality based in your truth. Your inner power is now supporting you in finding success and happiness while fulfilling your unique value and purpose. This higher realization of your Authentic Self guides and supports you in transcending the lower-based ego energy that created the false and limiting perceptions of your potential.

Remember, I previously stated that our spiritual truth must have some beneficial impact on our humanity in order to be relevant. Much of our past religious teachings have told us to believe or behave in a prescribed manner so that we can avoid a hellish afterlife. This tactic has imprinted great fear on many people, but it is man-made control, and not higher truth. Ultimately, we must align our energy to truth that supports us in leading loving and empowered lives.

If you try, you should easily notice all of the ways you previously held yourself back, or experienced great suffering while falsely defining a situation based on your egoic view.

Our minds are filled with a delusion that leads to disempowerment. With a higher identity you will learn to recognize value, healing, and growth even in situations that are challenging to your humanity.

This is because Spirit is Universal, unlimited, unconditional loving power. Ego is temporary, relating differently according to everyone's individual perspective, and it only functions in fear. *Shifting your identity is not a one-time declaration and action. It is the ongoing priority of your focused awareness in each present moment.* It is a practice – a spiritual practice.

Just like anything else you have endeavored to do well, you must have intention and you must practice. The more you function in your present loving energy, the more naturally and frequently you will reside in consciousness. This is your truth and highest state of being.

Above all else, on the human level this requires accountability. Your expressions of thoughts, words, feelings, and actions, are the energy that creates what and how you experience your external world. Therefore, you are accountable for all that you create. There is no more blaming others for your problems. Your problems now become your opportunities to see things differently, and to heal and grow. In this endeavor it is crucial that you identify with your Spirit instead of your ego. This leads to you to the opportunity to choose the energy of love over fear in all aspects and situations in your life.

You may be thinking that this cannot be easy. Most of us have been indoctrinated into our ego-training our whole lives, and are surrounded by those who, through ignorance or complacency, are relegating themselves to living in their lower identity. We have certainly had a great amount of practice in being human. But never forget that you are not this lower identity, you have the capabilities of Divinity. And you have the availability of inner guidance and support when you plug into your spiritual truth.

On the human level we utilize our WILL and determination to force a change in the conditions of our life. This reflects the intention for outer strength. The ego wants to control everything, and when possible, other people as well. We may change some condition or circumstance temporarily, but we have not addressed the inner cause that creates our problems to begin with. Therefore, we continue to re-create the same problem in different forms.

Through Spirit, our inspired path is to become WILLING to allow our light and truth to come through us with the insight, guidance, and support we need. This is the alignment of our life path with Source that offers the energy and qualities we need to begin to transform. With this willingness to be who we really are, our focus leads to living our real identity in each moment.

This is very different than identifying yourself as a "sinner" until a God "out there" helps or saves you. Do not abdicate your higher truth and power. That is clearly disempowering. You were created from Divinity to be and represent the Divine. Be accountable for creating your reality through your inner loving energy.

Mastering your life is about shifting to this higher identity and living your truth. You are here to live an enlightened path, an empowering human experience. Shifting your identity and realizing your Authentic Self will propel you to overcome ego training, heal from past false perceptions, develop mindfulness, and express love to all other beings. You will be supported in experiencing the Divine inner qualities of love, peace, joy, abundance, and wellness in all ways.

CHAPTER 5
Weakness Disguised as Strength

"The high minded man must care more for the truth than for what people think."

- Aristotle

Most of us learn how to live our life by observing those around us. They teach us our values and define our expectations. And this is designed to help us develop our own identity; it is to be a starting point. Yet, as we continue to look toward others for approval and affirmation, we often limit our potential and create disillusionment.

Our first priority has been to keep in step with the established parameters that our society dictates. Some of these rules help to protect us, and/or prepare us to function in the material world. Yet, when we are taking our marching orders from unconscious leadership we may find ourselves on a destructive path. We drink the Kool-Aid laced with ego-control and we become complicit in the cruelty and injustice all around us. And since many of the written and unwritten rules were established in the past by lesser evolved societies, they are based in fear and control. Maybe it's time some radical changes.

In order to awaken we must do more than just continue to pass along limitations, ignorance, and fear. The energy of life is always moving forward, shifting, changing, and progressing toward higher levels of consciousness. These ideals will be threatening to those who are all too comfortable within their superior place in the power struggle. From Jesus to Gandhi to Martin Luther King (and countless others) our history shows that often those with a higher view have been destroyed for daring to oppose those in power. Beginning with ourselves, let's start to do our part in elevating the consciousness in the world.

We learn well the lessons as children that to be different, independent, and contrary to the norms will lead to pain and suffering. This is taught to children by parents (directly or indirectly), and then reinforced in the school yard by these children. If the popular kids want to bully or pick on a kid who is different, disabled, or seemingly weaker, then you had better go along with the group. Otherwise you will receive the same harsh treatment. As adults we should know better, but instead, we just seem to continue this mindset of self-protection at all cost.

It is weakness disguised as strength. We're taught to just go along, don't make waves, and do what the people in power say to do. But I've got news for you, trying to follow all of the "rules," while neither understanding nor honoring your own true path and purpose will definitely lead you to pain and suffering. In the adult world this attitude prevails in most homes, work places, religions, law enforcement, governments, and relations between countries. Disconnection from our Authentic Self is a human problem regardless of social construct.

We are taught through fear to join into the masses who are striving for a position of power over others. This can mean anything from needing to be "right" in a conversation, to wielding political and financial clout in abusive ways. Within this struggle we create constant battles, where someone will feel defeated or victorious for a few minutes until the next ego-skirmish arises.

It is called survival of the fittest, and is the battle cry of our ego. While it is the lowest part of our nature, it has controlled the greatest part of our identity. And to what we attach our identity becomes the primary energetic space in which we will live our life. With everything being made up of energy, this is critical, and represents the need to "Awaken."

Simply watch the daily news, or listen to most any politician, preacher, or human dispute. Someone's a victim or a villain, right or wrong, good or evil; the delusion of duality is alive and well in the world today. The truth is that all of the energetic qualities that exist in the world lives within each of us.

In this world we have learned to judge the other guy, and if we do this loud enough, maybe we will avoid judgment against us. Political campaigns are often run this way. We learn to gain power over others by condemning them. And this is supposed to make us look more worthy and righteous by comparison. Most people do this all of the time, in one way or another. This is false power and represents ego (fear) and not Spirit (love).

The judgement that labels someone or something as "evil" exists first and foremost in our self-identification. What exists in our minds is later projected and manifested as the unloving examples of human behavior we see in the world. Therefore, we must be accountable for our own awakening and healing if we want to experience a better world.

The path of unconsciousness has been accepted in the world, and therefore, may seem harmless. Yet, it is undeniably unsupportive to your true empowerment, not to mention the welfare of others. It is blocking your light and higher connection. And when we continue to function in this way, we are energetically adding to the collective fear and darkness in the world.

If you are simply mimicking behaviors learned from others, you may be unconsciously choosing to experience your life out of fear, guilt, or harmful habit. Without a real inner connection to your own higher source, you are living your life based on cohabitation with your ego struggles. And you are also defining your value according to whether you are generally winning or losing your battles.

Do you have the "right" job, are you making "enough" money? Are you generally admired by others, do you meet the popular definition of beauty? Are you striving for the world's definition of success? This is the delusion that brings disempowerment and suffering, because it is judgment based on self-interest in comparisons with others.

All of this leads to great mental stress and anxiety about an unknowable, uncontrollable future that is presumably filled with lack and dangers of every kind. Fear, fear, and more fear. Someone who is truly empowered and inspired may actually find opportunities for higher contribution in all of this gloom and doom. But either way, when you are willing to awaken, you realize that your true identity is your Authentic Self, and not your ego.

You may in fact directly experience something harmful, hurtful, or unwanted. Yet, you can rightfully deal with these things most effectively from your strongest position of empowerment. The energy of fear (while occasionally motivating) is generally paralyzing and unsupportive.

Enlightened living asks you to be accountable to live and act from a position of love and inner strength. Besides, nearly all of the things that terrorize our minds will never actually be something we personally experience. We spend lifetimes agonizing, worrying, judging, and hating, for no reason other than ego-control and false identity. We are living within our own self-made prison.

In addition to this constant worldly education, your mind is always collecting data from all the input you have received. This includes not only the energy (thoughts, feelings, words, and actions) coming from others, but also how you interpreted this according to your limited ego perceptions. Without your Spirit identity as a compass, your mind is less reliable than you may think. You can easily get lost in your own delusions.

You are building a model of your self-image block by block, which may be "blocking" your highest energy. And, unfortunately, the way the ego works is to put more weight upon the information that was negative rather than positive. This is because ego is aligned with fear. It is always prepared to fight and defend its honor (so to speak), as you hang on to those hurtful energies, sometimes for decades.

People may insult you in any number of ways. You're lazy, stupid, unattractive, too big, too small, too poor, and too reserved or aggressive. Or you're a sinner, evil and in need of outside intervention, unworthy, and on and on it goes. These are merely other people's false judgments and opinions and nothing more.

Some of these people are merely misguided in their efforts to help you, while others are outright trying to help themselves by harming you. But regardless, even if their expressions resemble some quality or condition in your life, it has nothing to do with WHO you are. It is only their perception and assessment of you, and is, of course, based in their limited view of themselves and the world.

Does this offer a reasonable explanation as to why as humans we have become quite disempowered and lost? When all of our so-called power comes from other sources and not ourselves, we become reliant upon a myriad of external factors. On top of that, these outside sources are similarly controlled by their self-interest. We are all fighting for power because we think it is limited. We need to realize that it comes from our inner higher Source, and our job is not to capture it, but to let it flow through us.

We may blame God for our problems, or for not "saving" us. Or we blame other people for not being what we think they should be in order to help us. Once again, this is an example of why we must awaken to the realization of our Authentic Self.

Accepting and believing all of these false and limited teachings are not how you were designed to live. You're not this mindless, power-hungry, fear-based animal that the world teaches you to be. You are not a "winner," and therefore superior or entitled because you have more fortunate material conditions. If this was true it would imply that the have-nots are "losers," and therefore inferior. While this may be a popular ego-based opinion, it is false in the view of Spirit.

The truth is that in the "real" reality there is no duality. There are no winners or losers, nor superior or substandard people. There is only the perception that we are first and foremost our humanness which divides us, rather than Spirit which unites us. Each wave in the ocean is water, regardless of distinctions. In the same way, each person is Divine.

This is the great illusion that props up some people while denigrating others. This is all about ego, which holds us in fear. *And this is weakness not strength.* We must set the record straight; we are all equally worthy and capable of living our true power. Living connected to our Higher Self (Enlightened) is our original state of being, and therefore is available to all.

Mastering your life is about integrating your higher Authentic Self into your human experiences. It is not enough to take a few moments here and there to think or act in a "spiritual" way. It needs to be your central identity from which all human activities flow. And the process of enlightenment is how you become gradually more aware of this truth, and in your ability to live from this higher energetic space of being.

CHAPTER 6
Honoring Your Unique Life Path

The only time we suffer is when we believe a thought that argues with what is. When the mind is perfectly clear, "what is" is what we want."

- Byron Katie

You have chosen to come into this life, with your own unique purpose, gifts, qualities, and passions. This is a higher concept which reveals that our Spirit journey works together with our human experience. If on a higher level it was not beneficial for you to have your specific human life at this time then you wouldn't. And this is true, regardless of how you perceive your human conditions.

Just as true, when your purpose has been fulfilled and it is time to complete this experience and leave your body, it will be so. And this is true no matter when and how your body dies. Whether this human experience lasts one day or one hundred years, it serves your unique Spiritual purpose.

As part of realizing your Authentic Self you must fully accept your unique individual life path. This entails far more than the obvious physical distinctions. Sure, you have your own body, name, personality, and social security number. We can know from an early age the differentiation of our physical existence. However, your life path is about higher purpose, and your material attributes are simply the tools you have chosen to assist in your growth and development within this human experience. As Prince sang, "this thing called life."

Intellectually, it makes sense that we have our own lives which are different from that of other people. And certainly our focus has been on our own individual well-being above all other humans. Yet, we define the quality and value of our life in comparison to our perceptions of other people. And this is all based upon the arbitrary rules and opinions that were created in the ego world. This is not the realization of your Authentic Self.

We spend much time chasing the dreams of other people, and we moan and groan about the conditions or experiences we face. We continually say, "Why can't I have what they have?" And, "I don't like this situation, I want something better." Or worse, "I hate my life." This is evidence of our disconnection from our Authentic Self.

We are accepting that we have a distinct human life, but we do not own or honor our unique life path. We think that "bad" things happen TO us. Within our false identity we don't want to be accountable for creating our experiences. While disconnected from Spirit we are unaware that our journey always serves our higher purpose.

Our dissatisfaction leads us to more separation, isolation, and fear. This perspective is very disempowering and unsatisfying because ultimately we believe that we are never enough. And this fear-based belief pollutes all of our human endeavors to some degree.

Within whatever human constraints seem to apply to you, there is opportunity for you to be the best version of you. Endeavor to bring light instead of darkness to your sphere of influence in the world. Some lives will touch many and others relatively few; some lives last many more years than other lives; and some lives know greater wealth and physical health than others will know.

While we have learned to give so much weight to such human distinctions, in truth, they are merely examples of various unique life paths. They are not judgments as to a good or bad life. We all live our human experience for our own higher purpose, and all purposes are to be valued equally. When we can detach from ego perception, we can know that this is true.

I know that some of you may be saying, "Well this all sounds good, but how and why should I accept this as true? How can I just overlook the horrible injustice that I have experienced?" First, I would say you are not to overlook your experiences, but instead to accept what is. Don't deny it or resist it, but don't attach to it as your identity or value either.

When we attach our energy to our suffering we often will give away our power while endeavoring to defend our victimhood. This typically involves blaming others for your experiences, instead of focusing on the higher value to be gained. You are likely being led to healing, growth, and evolution in some form, but you will only notice this through accountability.

And second, you should not believe something just because I wrote it. Study this wisdom from your highest perspective. Regardless of how "difficult" it may seem to notice and live within this more enlightened perspective, you may recognize this as truth. It is the ongoing willingness to shift your energy toward love, and then begin to heal, grow, and ascend to your highest path.

Your current conditions simply make up a part of your life path; endeavor to accept this as a transitory energetic state. Be the noticer of your life, not one who is controlled by ego definitions and judgments. Instead of identifying with your conditions or experiences, examine them from a higher perspective. Learn to trust that everything is designed to support you in the Big Picture, and that you are empowered to create something more suited to your wellness. But you must be willing to take ownership of your life in order to be the master of it.

As you begin to awaken to the higher truth of realizing your Authentic Self, you are on a course to honor your unique life path. This connection to your spiritual essence is empowering and not subject to the world's delusion. In accepting that you are Spirit as well as physical human, you won't neglect your humanity. Instead, you can adopt a perspective that is supportive toward a higher fulfillment of both aspects of your being.

You may rightly say, "I am Spirit, and I chose this unique life path that includes the conditions and qualities that I am now experiencing, for the purposes of my higher growth, healing, and evolution." On a human/ego scale these can be perceived as either ideal or not, however, the truth is that this is the reality you are experiencing, so you want to eliminate judgment and delusion.

How this life compares to anyone else is really irrelevant. Your job is to accept what is, and then claim your greatest power to make the choices or take the actions that are most supportive to your well-being. This is Enlightened Living.

From our collective human perspective we experience all possible life paths. No one person is less significant than another; we all matter equally. The only relevant distinction that has any merit is our level of consciousness. For this will determine our ability to express the quality of love to us and others, regardless of our human conditions. Our job, income, looks, or popularity is really just temporary window dressing.

Our population of humans makes up the total opportunity for our world of Souls to evolve. It also provides for the full spectrum of loving service in caring for the world's inhabitants. However, thus far we have largely chosen a more unawakened and selfish path, and this is evidence of not honoring our truth.

From your own individual perspective you must live this life within the unique path you chose. This is your truth, your Authentic Self. You can fight, hate, or try to ignore it, but in the end you must eventually face your own truth. And the sooner you can do this, the more effective you will be toward living a more conscious fulfilling human experience.

Once again, the key to self-mastery is in accepting your unique life path as intentionally designed by you, and then being accountable for living it with as much love and empowerment as you can. Your life is not a mistake or curse. It is absolutely on target for fulfilling your higher purpose. You start from where you begin in this life. However, from there, a masterful person will best utilize their specific gifts, qualities, and purpose to live within the higher energy of love and service.

Examples of Accepting your Truth

Most of us are not raised with a silver spoon or born into complete poverty. We are typically brought up somewhere in between and then attract various experiences that feel good or bad from our ego perspective. In addition to the discussion above, there are unlimited examples of where accepting our truth leads to enlightened living. Let me give you a couple of scenarios that may pertain to you personally or guide you in understanding.

Aging Happens, Accept It

Usually, when we are young we want the things we think being older will give us, and we are impatient for something we perceive as more valuable. And when we are older we desire some of the attributes of youth, we long for qualities we believe we once possessed. By focusing on our life this way, we are not accepting what is. Our delusion is setting us up for unhappiness.

As I am writing this book I am 55 years old, I have friends in their 60's and parents in their 70's. Whether through personal example or through my close associations I am beginning to understand how the body begins to break down as compared to our younger bodies.

For my part I do the things I can do physically, like working out regularly, meditating daily, eating better, and getting physical checkups. As for what is outside of my control, I accept this as the current part of my life path. I am choosing not to add unnecessary stress and dissatisfaction by wishing things to be different than they are. This would only create more problems. And, I am choosing to acknowledge with appreciation all of the amazing blessings that only exist in this present time in my life, thereby, creating more of them.

I have observed that those who have experienced great ego gratification from their youth, due to their relative physical prowess or beauty, often have much regret around getting older. When our ego has garnered significant power from our human characteristics, we inevitably feel all the more powerless when these qualities are diminished. The problem is not in getting older, it is in identifying with ego and not Spirit. Therefore, we tend to judge ourselves as having less value, or are reminded of our mortality. This fear is always the byproduct of ego. And no one is going to add days to their lifespan through the delusion of ego.

Yet, if we are more awakened, we will find fulfillment in the value which lies in our present truth. Our inner qualities do not diminish, and actually may be more greatly developed. Things like, acceptance, peace, joy, love, compassion, wisdom, etc. This is the connection to our Authentic Self, which leads to our more holistic wellness. We are energy, and energy always moves and shifts. The acceptance of what is leads to the acceptance of our higher truth. At all ages and stages of life, enlightened living supports the balancing of the quality of our spiritual and physical wellness.

Life Throws You a Curve

Here is another example of the value of accepting your life path. We all have many times where there is the sudden shifting from our life going relatively smoothly to more turbulent or devastating circumstances. As energy naturally flows and opportunities for growth continue to "support" us. And we create new situations that require some changes, shifting, or deeper understanding and inner healing.

This will often feel unwanted or harsh on a human/ego level. Most often this will be connected to some actions or involvement with another person; otherwise, it might come as a sudden ailment. Did you ask for that person to manipulate and abuse you, or for your job to go away, or for that accident or illness? Depending upon your acceptance of full accountability for your life path, you may not want to know the answer to that question. But either way, your humanity did not want to deal with this.

Nevertheless, you are thrown headlong into a challenging situation from which you must continue to operate your overall life. When controlled by ego we will fight against the thing that happened to us, blame others, and then resist this new reality. No one is asking you to be happy about something that initially causes pain and suffering. Yet happy or not, this is what you got.

You may not yet be able to make sense of this as a benefit to you on your unique life path. However, you must do your best to apply the following principle: Everything that happens to/for me is on some level necessary and beneficial for my higher growth and evolution. Initially, this is the "faith" part. In any case, your mind can at least understand that for the days, months, or years that you spend complaining, resisting, and blaming, you are not effectively living your greater joy, love, and fulfillment.

CHAPTER 7

Your Initial Human Circumstances

"I am not what happened to me, I am what I choose to become."

- C. G. Jung

You have chosen the details of your physical, mental, and emotional makeup, as well as your family, nationality, race, gender, etc. In doing this, you have setup the conditions from which you must transcend and evolve, in order to achieve some aspect of spiritual growth and service to others. Additionally, as Spirit (before incarnation) you have "contracted" with certain key individual souls in order to share some significant experiences that serve your growth or karmic resolution.

When I talk about accepting your life path, this includes the conditions in which you began this life, the things you were born with. I know that for some, this is a very challenging concept. Your initial circumstances also include your related potentialities. For instance, you were obviously born a human baby, however, your DNA projects to define your physical, mental, and emotional characteristics in this life.

On some level you must accept your truth within this human potential. For me, even though as a kid I loved playing basketball, I have topped out around 5'-8". Therefore, no amount of wishing was going to lead me to a career as a professional basketball player. Yet, that does not mean that I do not have great potential in accepting and developing the gifts I do have.

This may sound like a silly example. Nevertheless, how often have we all created much suffering and unhappiness because we weren't willing to accept the truth of a situation? However, this is not a directive to give up on your dreams. When you believe that you are aligned with your true purpose and unique qualities, give it your best shot.

Your initial conditions and circumstances always offer potential for your growth and accomplishment that is in alignment with your true purpose. We likely won't understand the true value of our unique path and surroundings early in life. Even if you are experiencing challenges greater than that of many other people, it is for you to ascend in a way that honors your truth. Accepting your life path and facilitating the healing, growth, and evolution that supports you is the only meaningful objective from the standpoint of enlightenment.

The value and worthiness of a human life cannot rightfully be defined or judged according to its initial circumstances. Whatever your conditions are, they are perfect for you. Your highest achievement involves personal growth and service to others, your greatest value comes from contribution. Again, regardless of the perceived human qualities, what matters most is honoring your inner truth as you heal, grow, and evolve within your unique human experience.

Start with the acceptance of your higher value, apart from your human conditions. Next, explore and understand your unique gifts from a more objective, empowering space. What do you enjoy doing or experiencing? As the acclaimed American teacher Joseph Campbell instructs, "Find your bliss." Discover what feels natural and inspiring to you. How do your specific conditions, circumstances, or qualities translate into a purpose for serving the world?

As you discover your truth you will be positioned to utilize all of your power to support your best path. As you awaken, you shift to a higher perspective of what is possible. You may begin to direct your thoughts, words, feelings, and actions toward more loving expressions for all. Then start to design a path, and take the steps you need in order to proceed toward your goals. Everything is a process of discovery and the unfolding of possibilities.

These goals are determined by you according to your inner guidance, as opposed to following the crowd and trying to reach outcomes that are not in alignment with your truth. Trust your Authentic Self and forge your own path. To paraphrase the poet Robert Frost, this is the road less traveled, which makes all of the difference.

CHAPTER 8

Great Value in All
of Your Experiences

*"If you change the way you look at things,
the things you look at change."*

- Dr. Wayne W. Dyer

On the human level, your experiences may be perceived by ego as joyful or painful, positive or negative. Yet on a soul level they offer great assistance by demonstrating on the physical plane the status of the energy that is emanating from within us. And this relates to our wellness on a holistic level – body, mind, and spirit.

By the way, when I use the term experiences, I am including your reactions in terms of thoughts and feelings surrounding the thing that has taken place. Many times are experiences involve some interaction with another person. Therefore, you will deal with the impact of their energy as well as your own. Yet, it is only your energy that you are empowered to work with.

When connected more fully with your Authentic Spiritual Self you will be more in tune with your expressions of energy. However, when you get lost in ego, and disconnected from Spirit, you may need an external experience to show up to let you know what is going on energetically. Within a more enlightened view, we manifest our experiences in order to regain our awareness of the quality of our energetic wellness, and to reclaim our power.

One of the great challenges of being human lies in determining what experiences are stop signs, redirects, or opportunities to push through with trust and persistence. Your ego may simply continue to bring up your inner doubt and fear, depending upon the accumulation of input throughout your life. Some people have attached to a negative self-belief in a very debilitating way. In this case, their fear may cause them to shy away from challenges or abandon their dreams prematurely.

A great value in awakening to your higher truth is that you will create opportunities through mindfulness to evaluate these situations on a deeper level. You will have the wisdom to recognize your inner fear, as opposed to simply being overwhelmed by it. Now you may decide on a course of action that honors your truth. Regardless of specifics, your challenge may actually be – are you going to honor your truth? Or if your strong inner knowing is that you need to redirect in some way, at least you are now making this decision based in wisdom and not fear.

I have personally encountered this in my life. As one who was more comfortable behind the scenes and not making waves, it was not easy for me to speak my truth. However, when opportunities came along that were non-confrontational, I was quite effective at sharing wisdom with others in support of them. This whole process of writing and speaking my truth has been preceded by great inner transformation.

Many times I have been challenged by the old fear that this idea of pursuing my dream as an author/teacher was irrational or impossible. Through experience, my awareness was showing me where I was still connected to ego and fear. Yet, my Spirit connection continued to encourage me to keep going.

This is a gradual process of healing and growth, and it takes intention and effort. I have been guided to create my own path within this work that honors my truth, as opposed to trying to emulate someone else. You can do the same thing in your life.

Sometimes, even while being relatively conscious, we will attract experiences that will teach or guide us to shift some behavior or perception. We may be attracting some new energy that supports us moving in a different direction. Tune in to see how this "feels." We first want to examine our energy, and accept the truth of the situation. As we are able to remain unattached to what we may have thought "should be," and honor our present knowing, we will more quickly accept the change and receive the benefit.

At other times, if we are not picking up the cues to release attachment (fear) and move in a new more empowering direction for the sake of our wellness, we will be in need of a less subtle event to get our attention. This often manifests as a more challenging experience; and the greater our lack of awareness the greater the probability of suffering on some level.

Since our primary focus was on ego and not Spirit, we missed the more subtle inner hints that were exclaiming our higher truth. In addition to present moment awareness, our accumulation of lessons from past experiences was opportunities to assist our current judgment. Had we been more open to Spirit or healing from our past, we would not have created a particularly challenging experience.

This clearly happens to each of us when, for example, we feel locked into a relationship or job that no longer serves our best interests. Yet for the sake of comfort, familiarity, and fear of the unknown, we stay in this situation longer than we should. Your spirit will lovingly give you the impetus to shift directions. In human terms this could be a painful breakup or a job termination, which may feel punitive to your ego. Yet in truth, it is redirecting you to a higher path, as you were unaware of your need to do this of your own conscious choosing.

We attract our experiences to awaken and support us to heal, grow, and evolve. The majority of our human suffering rarely comes from the actual event, even though it may be hurtful and fearful at the time. By far the greatest suffering takes place beyond the actual event when we are resisting the lesson and value of the experience as the awakening opportunity that it is.

Our ignorance and fear causes much human misery and it doesn't have to be. Worse yet is that we create this misery for ourselves and then we dump it on other people. Instead of doing this, we can choose to accept, and then realize the value of all of our experiences. While living in our truth we may transcend our challenges and recognize great benefit. Again, this is how we become masters of our life.

CHAPTER 9
Energetic Cause and Effect

"Happiness is not a reward – it is a consequence. Suffering is not a punishment – it is a result."

- Robert Green Ingersol

At times we go through life, tossed about and roughed up by our ego perceptions of what we think "should be." We become engulfed by a negative energy that affects us quite adversely. You can actually see and feel the difference between people who express gratitude and kindness versus those who spew resentment and anger.

In truth, the circumstances between these people need not be any different from each other. One has attached to the ego perception of fear and says, "Why is the world always dumping on me?" They are looking and judging outside of themselves, and they are wishing for someone or something to heal or save them.

The other person in the above example is recognizing an inner connection to their spiritual nature (whether or not they are using that terminology). Therefore, they are building upon the energy that is allowing a more positive and optimistic outlook. They are accepting their truth and defining their value from within. They will always be more empowered to create higher energetic experiences.

When they talk about our words being a self-fulfilling prophecy it is because all things are made of and created by energy. If we are stuck in a negative perception pattern we

73

strongly need an awakening to a higher truth. This, then, may shift us to the creation of more loving experiences.

If you say, "look at me, I am poor, lonely, unhealthy, and unsatisfied with this life, and instead of that, I want to be rich, loved by others, and physically healthy." I want "that" and not "this" does not change your energy or physical reality when it is based in fear. You are wishing for a magic pill that does not exist.

You must connect to your Authentic Self, and focus on shifting your perception of your life. Seek to express energy that is supportive in creating the conditions you desire. Never say "I am this," if "this" is something you do not want to be or create. Like all energy, your words are powerful, therefore, always be mindful.

It is not that the less conscious person is bad (though they may be judged that way by others) and therefore deserves negative experiences. It is not about judgment at all. It is simply that through their energy they continue to create their negativity.

There is energetic cause and effect here. Spirit is trying to show them the need for awakening and shifting. Additionally, like energy draws unto itself. Therefore, an angry person attracts someone to make them angrier; a fearful person attracts someone (or something) to make them more fearful. While a loving person more easily attracts opportunities to love; and a peaceful person more often finds the conditions of peace.

When conscious, these are all choices. When you are relatively unconscious and controlled by ego you likely will be unaware of your true accountability for all that shows up in your life. This is often very frustrating and disempowering.

Once we have the awareness to recognize that we are always getting what we attract, we will elevate our energetic expressions to attract what we want. And even when we do not fully understand why we attracted an experience or situation, we more easily can accept what shows up as part of our truth yet to be defined. All of this supports us in living more enthusiastically and empowered

Being the master of your life requires that you live within the mindset that you are creating the causes of your empowered reality through your energy. Therefore, you more easily take responsibility for your thoughts, words, feelings, and actions. Now you may know and accept that your life unfolds according to your energetic expressions, and not the whims or unconsciousness of other people.

CHAPTER 10
Identifying with the Light of Your Truth

"Every man can easily forgive a child who is afraid of the dark; the real tragedy of life is when men are afraid of the light."

- Plato

As I have stated several times, on the level of Spirit you chose your unique life path, including all of your conditions, gifts, qualities, passions, and purpose. You chose the parameters of the overall lessons that would be most supportive to the evolution of your Soul. And therefore, your circumstances and specific human qualities play an integral role in your life path and Soul journey. Regardless of how it is perceived by your ego, everything fits the purpose of your development and evolution. And your Authentic Self knows this as the light of your truth.

Your higher purpose in this life is to discover and apply your own unique qualities and circumstances in the sharing of your light and loving energy. If you are presently unable to do this, then you are not in alignment with your true identity. This is not a criticism, it is simply truth. You are meant to support your own evolution, as well as that of humanity. You cannot do this while dishonoring your truth. You must not hide your light or attempt to live someone else's path.

This is a really difficult concept for many people. You have been taught your whole life what is right or wrong for you, do this not that, and be this don't be that. All of the while your Authentic Self knows exactly who you are, and what is right for you. At some point there is an element of connecting within and releasing the noise, distraction, and false teaching coming from outside of you. Yet, your self-mastery will be an ongoing process of inner acceptance.

If on some level you chose this path on Earth, regardless of how it may be judged by others, don't you have an obligation to your higher self to at least explore it for the value it may offer? Ultimately, it does no good to live in the perception of lack, disempowerment, and disappointment. In truth this is a choice to identify with ego. And it is futile to blame a God outside of yourself, or other people for your challenges. You are not a mistake or failure, merely misguided. What you call challenges may best be overcome by honoring your truth.

You need not expect any outside source to "save" you, because you are living within the conditions that you established for your own higher purposes. And when you shift your perspective and awareness toward discovering and applying your highest truth, you may find the personal accountability and power you need. You may now accept your higher identity.

This is the releasing of ego identification that was blocking you from transcending your perceived challenges. Connected to Spirit you are open to the inner guidance that redirects or otherwise leads you to solutions that are in alignment with your unique path and purpose.

What is always available and most supportive is to place your intentions upon an awakening to the uniquely designed purpose that you are here to fulfill. In other words, go within, to elevate your connection (awareness) to your Authentic Self, and ask the following type questions. What am I being taught by the experiences I am attracting? How may I gain my greatest empowerment in utilizing these lessons? How may I transform to a higher state of being or enlightenment? What is my highest purpose in service to the world? And, how may I perceive and express the energy of love in all of my human circumstances and interactions?

Most people have been unwilling to accept this level of accountability for their lives, but the process of self-mastery requires it. The reason why we need to consciously and intentionally connect to this higher part of ourselves is because we have been systematically taught and encouraged to live in our lower awareness. And while attached to our human ego perspective, we lose sight of our truth. Then, with the free will that followed us into this human experience, we make choices that further attach us to our *untruth*. Through countless repetitions of this practice, including the constant bombardment of false teachings and negative energy from others, we become unconscious as to our true identity.

Each of us has special gifts, qualities, and passions that may be explored and developed into the skillset that expresses our purpose in this physical world. And each of your experiences and interactions provide an opportunity for you to acknowledge and honor your Authentic Self and express your true power. We connect to our inner truth every time we awaken to our higher awareness in the present moment. By the way, our meditation practice helps us develop this skill and habit by shifting our focus inward.

Is your awareness confirming that you are in this moment identifying with Spirit? You will know this to be true if you are expressing love in one form or another. Or is your awareness presently confirming your attachment to ego? You will know this to be true if you are expressing fear in one form or another.

Regardless of your choices on this life path, your Spirit can never leave you, for it is not separate from you. Instead, it is your identification with your lower self that causes you to lose the awareness of this Presence. And for however your choices manifest in the material world, Spirit is trying to teach or show you where you are aligned.

In this human experience we are never going to be completely detached from ego. Therefore, by awakening to our truth, combined with our consistent spiritual practice, we may gradually shift to more often identify with Spirit through higher consciousness.

This is why there is always a part of you that has an occasional knowing, a flicker of insight, or hint about what is your highest truth. Something you've dreamed of doing or being. Not because it is popular, or highly compensated, but because it just "feels" right for you on a deeper level. Live in this awareness to create your greatest joy, fulfillment, and contribution.

Sometimes, "out of nowhere" you are suddenly pulled toward unexpected selfless integrity and compassion. The key is to remain present and follow through with your higher insight, before your ego talks you out of it by introducing fear. More often trust your first instincts. As you get more consistent about being mindful and claiming your power (which is the basis of Part II in this book) you will be guided back to your truth more often.

Your highest purpose is to grow, transform, and evolve on a spiritual level. Your human experiences are the tools to achieve your higher goals. The term "Authentic Self" should indicate to you the idea of your "True Self," and that your human qualities are a temporary expression of your unique and exclusively designed Soul purpose.

You should know that, for whatever conditions you find yourself, you are as valuable and worthy as anyone else who has ever chosen to experience a human life. You simply have a different mission. However, if you are living unconsciously, you are unaware of any higher identity, purpose, or plan. Your focus is likely on merely surviving and functioning within the delusion of ego. You are trying to "solve problems" instead of creating your best life.

We each have our own higher purpose within the lives we have chosen. Maybe those who have come here to experience less are giving those of us with much, an opportunity to be more giving and compassionate. This is higher wisdom that supports the well-being of all.

The full extent of any explanation or justification for our spiritual journey and life path is unknowable in human terms. I am sorry if that statement is unsatisfying to your intelligence. Most often our perception has been limited to both our physical senses and the thoughts we have been taught to believe. Within this book series I am sharing some wisdom that may require a bit of faith, but is likely more supportive to your holistic well-being than much of what has been accepted in the world.

I hope that humankind will begin to consider that everything in existence has a higher purpose. For the sake of identifying with the light of your truth you must allow for the opportunity to explore and realize a positive potentiality in all situations. From this perspective you live more awakened, and connected to your Authentic Self.

Those who realize and honor their Authentic Self earlier in life seem to thrive with an inner confidence and knowing as to their purpose in service to the world. However, most of us will move along the life path destined to learn from our experiences according to our ego education. Eventually at some point, we may develop a greater awareness of the consequences of our choices. And we may recognize the promises of the world to be delusion and fools gold. This will then motivate us to awaken to our higher truth.

A significant part of our journey is in transcending our initial circumstances as a way of growing and transforming into our true power. This is likely the more common way that most of us will evolve. You make this shift according to your level of consciousness. Whenever you are ready to awaken is perfect for you, this is not a competition, and each Soul is unique.

At some point on our journey we stop all of this blind ambition, constant striving, outward aggression, and seeking the approval of others. We decide that we are ready to connect with and listen to our inner voice. We begin to choose love over fear much more often, for the betterment of all life. Maybe you, too, are ready to identify with your Authentic Self.

And then a picture forms, showing you the truth of who you are, and what you are here to offer the world. And you realize that you have been loved, guided, and protected all along. When you can reach this place in life with love for your journey instead of regret and judgment, you can transition into a full acceptance of your light.

You have always been part of the Universal Life Force that has created all things. Own and accept your life and everything that you have experienced as part of your unique path to understanding and growth. This is the level of accountability that will change your life from the inside out. Now the power of the present moment will support you in connecting to a higher reality. From there your energy can be placed on gratitude for the opportunity of life, and also on the guidance that supports you in taking steps in the present to benefit yourself and others.

Sometimes these may be very small steps, but progress is progress, so don't judge. When you are more willing to help yourself, more opportunities will appear in which others may assist you. As you gain a higher perspective on your life you will be more available to show kindness or offer loving service to other people.

Now you are living your unique life path in a way that is more joyful and fulfilling. You may still be relatively poor, alone, and unhealthy (as compared to some others). Yet you may also be able to experience these same outer conditions that previously brought much suffering, with inner strength, peace, empowerment, and gratitude. You are now on the way to mastering your life, and living enlightened!

PART I: Exercises

1) Describe three significant events or experiences from your past that may have caused you to question your value or identity.

2) How do the experiences in #1 look different from the perspective of your ego-based identity versus your Spirit-based identity? Through higher awareness are you able to rise from victim to empowerment as you recognize a higher truth and purpose for the experience?

3) Describe at least five qualities that you can identify (gifts, talents, special interests, or passions) that represent your truth and may support you in fulfilling a higher purpose on your unique life path?

PART I: Affirmations

I AM a spiritual being having a human experience.

I AM living my inner truth and higher purpose.

I AM perfectly designed to live my truth.

I AM Spirit and I chose my unique life path.

I AM empowered to live my highest consciousness.

I AM expressing my higher truth in all of my experiences.

I AM always enough.

I AM the Master of my life.

I AM the Light of my Truth.

I AM now expressing the loving energy of my Authentic Self.

I AM awakening to my highest life path.

PART II:

CLAIMING YOUR PRESENT MOMENT POWER

"The secret of health for both mind and body is not to mourn for the past, worry about the future, or anticipate troubles, but to live in the present moment wisely and earnestly."

- Buddha

PART II: **Prologue**

Ultimately, enlightened living supports us in utilizing the higher power available to us from the realization of our Authentic Self. Therefore, this is the true power from Spirit, and not the false perception of power we have often pursued in the many sources outside of ourselves. Self-Mastery involves claiming your present moment power, as this represents a connection to Spirit through mindfulness.

When your focus is on honoring your true self you will also honor all of your experiences as an empowering part of your life path. Present moment focus and intention supports you in expressing your energy (thoughts, feelings, words, and actions) from the quality of love. When we lack mindfulness and Presence we will habitually defer to our ego training in fear. We then suffer within the perceptions and delusions of our mind, which may hold us prisoner with disempowering false beliefs from the past.

When conscious in the present, we know that the past has served to offer the teaching experiences we needed at the time. Therefore, we more easily release this energy and shift to that which is most loving and supportive today. At times we will revert to our fearful perceptions of the past, or agonize over what may come or not come in the future. Yet, when we are conscious, we may utilize our awareness and reset our mental focus to the present to once again be as loving and productive as possible. Instead of wanting, wishing, and worrying about things being different than they are, a satisfying future is ultimately created by your power in the present.

PART II: Energetic Quality or Tool

For the sake of Claiming your Present Moment Power, a key Divine Energetic Quality or Tool you will need is *AWARENESS*. You may have already picked up that each new moment becomes the next present moment. The goal is to be continuously attentive of your mind and the quality of your energy.

This is applicable regardless of the myriad of physical or mental activities in which you may be involved. Awareness is the overriding ingredient or quality to support a "mindful" connection to the present moment. Should we lose our focus and become unconscious (disconnected from higher truth), it is awareness that brings us back to our power. This is a potent tool that must be developed, hence the purpose of practices like meditation.

The Divine energy of Awareness is opposed by your ego mind, which has likely controlled your mental state through the opposite qualities of *IGNORANCE* or *UNCONSCIOUSNESS*. This indicates that we have attached our identity to ego, and have chosen or allowed our minds to be influenced by this delusion. We are unwilling to perceive things in a more loving or enlightened truth. Without mindfulness, our minds often wander endlessly in ways that will energetically create negative experiences and a disempowering perspective.

Once you awaken to your Authentic Self, you know that you are greater than your ego thoughts and human circumstances. The next progression in mastery is to gain the power of the present moment that allows you to love and honor your true life path and purpose as you are living it.

CHAPTER 11

Divine Presence in the Present Moment

"Unease, anxiety, tension, stress, worry – all forms of fear – are caused by too much future, and not enough presence. Guilt, regret, resentment, grievance, sadness, bitterness, and all forms of non-forgiveness are caused by too much past, and not enough presence."

- Eckhart Tolle

The one indisputable truth about Enlightened Living is that it is an intention and practice that takes place in each present moment. Otherwise we will act enlightened in one moment and unconscious in the next. A wonderful goal for each of us is to develop the kind of mindfulness and awareness where we gradually increase the amount of time we are conscious and present. While there is an aspect of dedication to your practice, it really becomes more about living connected to your higher truth.

It is more about allowing and accepting than forcing and controlling. This is the difference between Spirit identification and ego identification. This necessitates an awakening and shifting of perceptions that guide and support you in being more present. When you can function within this space you are connected to your Divine Presence.

As you are more alive and connected within each new present moment, you have the power of choice and the ability to assess your level of energy. You may notice your thoughts and feelings connected to any particular human activity or interaction. You may maintain the inner strength and peace to evaluate your words and actions before they might cause a problem.

You are in your greatest power while surrounded by Divine Presence in the present moment. This is not some force outside of you. This is being accountable for your higher expressions of energy. This is your Soul connecting to your humanity. Knowing that it is our energetic expressions that manifest as our experiences, you can see how significant this is.

Within your truth, your mind is not stuck in some past drama or distraction. You are not denying or discounting the future, but you are more positive with your thoughts and more productive with your actions now. This will be most supportive in creating the future that you truly desire.

Of course, when we are disconnected from our Authentic Self in the present moment, we are disempowered within the ego energy of fear. Our ego wants to control everything in our lives, which is impossible. We experience mental stress and anxiety for all of the imagined future outcomes that we don't want to experience. We become stagnant while pondering the questions about our future for which we presently have no answers. Or we may be lost in some past experience that either felt good or bad to our ego, but either way does not exist now.

Does being present and conscious mean that in each moment we feel happy and have everything go our way? No, it does not. It is true, however, that ultimately we will create more positive, supportive opportunities and experiences than before when we were controlled more often by ego. Yet, we are human and therefore not free from ego. And regardless of our higher perspective and energy, we continue to deal with real human issues that are surrounded by lower energy.

Our energy will ebb and flow as life moves forward. We continue to interact with many unconscious people, and therefore, will encounter negative energy from time to time. Our bodies will manifest illness or disease on occasion, and some days we will feel stronger than other days.

Here is a major advantage for cultivating your Divine Presence in each present moment - regardless of your external experience, you have access to awareness and wisdom which offer positive choices in support of your wellness. Since we are noticing our energy levels we may then be accountable for adjusting the expression and usage of our energy. This is self-regulation (and self-mastery) that is only possible when conscious.

If we feel run down with lower energy, for whatever reason, we may take actions that require less energetic output. Maybe this leads to more rest, or the shifting of our thoughts, feelings, and responsibilities to something more positive and supportive than what we would normally have dealt with. Conversely, when our energy is stronger, we may take on a more assertive position or be better prepared to deal with challenging opportunities or interactions.

If someone approaches us with great negativity, we will now have a space of awareness that reminds us to remain in Spirit. We know that whatever they are expressing is their energy, and we have a choice to attach to it or not. Our Presence will choose to remain empowered within, and respond in an appropriate way without encouraging an ego battle. Otherwise, while unconscious we likely become offended and return the attack.

Being present turns our free will into a tool for enlightened living. While being unconscious deprives us of this higher tool. Thereby, we revert to our past ego training and habitual self-serving objectives. Since we are now endeavoring to integrate our Authentic Self into our humanity, it should be becoming clear that we can only successfully accomplish this by living our Divine Presence in the present moment. And our intention is to do this as frequently as possible.

Connected to our Divinity, we have access to the higher qualities we desire. We want to express and attract love, peace, joy, abundance, wellness, fulfillment, and meaning. These are now more readily available. Our present moment power also includes the quality of creation or creativity. These are examples of the great power to be claimed in the present moment.

I am writing these words and pages of this book in this present moment. I am connected to my Authentic Self, which is the aspect of Divine Presence that is guiding me now. Tomorrow's writing will take place in a different present moment. However, my intentions are to find my truth in whatever present moment I am living.

The key is that there is tremendous focus, power, and support when connected and functioning in this way. This is the same for you in whatever activity or purpose in which your Authentic Self is guiding you to experience. When you are in this space you will naturally feel that you are in the flow of your highest energy, you are connected to your bliss.

You do not have to "create" writing, art, or music to be connected to Divine Presence in the present moment. You can experience this power in anything that you do in which you give your true and highest energy and integrity. This is the mindfulness training you have likely heard of before. You can be present while walking, cleaning, eating, talking, working, etc. This is why success and fulfillment are always about experiencing this Presence. It is more about how you do things, and not just the outcome.

As it relates to offering this energy to others, our great joy comes from what we give, and not just what we get. The "getting" comes directly from the giving when it involves your Divine Presence. Have you ever noticed how many things we do half-heartedly? Or we give our labor or resources begrudgingly? Or even when our motivation is wrapped up in self-interest? This is not fulfilling or rewarding on a level that satisfies your

Authentic Self. Even if it garners money and accolades, you are not honoring your truth. When we are not living our Presence we are disconnected from our Spirit, and wasting the power of the present moment.

It is up to us to fully engage in life, which is the point of awakening! We have so much to offer, and are only truly fulfilled when in this space of Presence. As you begin to heal and shift your awareness and perspective of life, you will take responsibility for connecting to your higher truth and then choosing what is most meaningful to you. And when you are living your life empowered in this way, you will recognize success and joy in whatever it is you are doing. You are Mastering Your Life!

CHAPTER 12

Transcending Ego-Mind
through Awareness

"When we quit thinking primarily about ourselves and our own self-preservation, we undergo a truly heroic transformation of consciousness."

- Joseph Campbell

In the moments in which we are not living in our Presence, we are attached to the ego-delusion in our minds. Attachment is a form of identification that takes control over our perceptions and removes us from our connection to the present moment. While identifying with our minds we are limited to the whims, endless "rabbit trails" and to-do lists, and the concerns of the ego. When we sink into this space of mind we may be sent to whatever particular disempowering thought, feeling, or experiential translation of the past where ego is drawn.

We can easily get lost in our heads, and miss the moment with our relentless undisciplined thinking. Sometimes our thoughts stray toward the anxiety of an unknown future, which may leave us feeling powerless. A future made all the more fearful as we routinely live unconscious and unproductive in the present moments that lead us to and help create our future. And those of us who have lived more than a few decades understand how fast time moves, and how important it is to not waste the opportunities we have in the present.

Stuck in our unconsciousness we miss the inspiration, peace, love, focus, enthusiasm, insight, and joy that is possible. We block out our connection to Spirit, our highest state of being. Yet, when we are linked to our power we can best utilize our brain, body, feelings, and Spirit as it relates to the present. This is an empowering reality.

When we live a masterful life we integrate all aspects of ourselves in order to gain the most from each moment. Sometimes this calls for rest and silence, and other times activity and effort. We can allow for whatever is in that moment, without wishing it to be different. We apply our highest forces for the best result. No wasted effort or forays into needless mental gymnastics or suffering.

As humans, we are likely to spend much time in our head. We are thinking, analyzing, planning, manipulating, judging, etc. There is a great need for us to be more balanced and connected to heart (Spirit) as well as head. Our energy is best linked to our spiritual truth in this way, because it is more authentic to feel your power than to think it. It is also more productive to be empowered to take steps in the direction of our goals, rather than to simply *think* about doing something. This is not meant to dismiss the value of analysis and planning while attached to our Presence. In fact this can be a part of the creative process.

The point is to develop your higher awareness to notice when you are living in your mind, disconnected from Spirit. And then to shift your focus back to your Presence in order to live more enlightened. This is the on-going value of intention and practice that assists you in transcending ego-delusion. It is awareness overcoming ignorance, and it is the path to self-mastery.

CHAPTER 13

Your Power Lies in the Present Moment

"Realize deeply that the present moment is all you ever have. Make the now the primary focus of your life."

- Eckhart Tolle

There are two primary reasons why the present moment is powerful. First, this is the only time we are conscious and connected to life. Therefore, we can only live in the present moment; nothing else exists. And, existence is powerful, while non-existence is powerless.

The past is only a memory of a previous present moment. You have no power to affect change there. The future consists of yet-to-be-lived present moments. And while they may represent an unlimited number of potentialities, none of them can be directly experienced today. All of your power lies in the present moment.

Every present moment spent stuck in some past drama or future deliberation is a moment lived unconsciously. If we are to be the masters of our life we must endeavor to live in the space of our greatest power. We must become more mindful and present.

The second reason why the present moment is quite powerful is that energy is constantly shifting and changing, both within us and all around us. And therefore, we must be present in order to more fully adapt to the "what is" that exists in our life, as it is occurring. With this higher focus of our energy we will experience our life with greater meaning and value. We can accept all that is presently manifesting and unfolding.

In this present moment we may find conditions to be varying degrees of peaceful. While in the next present moment we may encounter more fear-based energies. These could either be independently arising within us based on some false self-belief, or they could be directed from an outside source that touched upon a personal ego trigger.

We should look at this ebb and flow of energy as a natural occurrence. Nothing is always smooth or turbulent; we are constantly in a state of growth and flux. This corroborates an earlier comment when I said that we are never once-and-for-all-time secure in a state of enlightenment, at least not within our human experience.

The energy of life moves to bring us what we need to learn, experience, or contribute in each new present moment. We attract this as a by-product of how we express our energy (in thoughts, words, feelings, and actions), and also as a reflection of our Soul's purpose. In order to live "enlightened," we understand that the quality of the energy we express will create the quality of our experiences. Therefore, our greatest power comes from utilizing our present moments to hold a loving space.

The concept that, whether for "good or bad," we create our circumstances and experiences is often hard for people to accept. Our ego prefers to take credit for the things that feel good, but is far less inclined to take responsibility for the negative aspects of our life. Instead, we have been conditioned to blame others. Or we inflict negativity upon ourselves in a way that is self-defeating. This non-accountability and dishonoring of our truth is ultimately disempowering, and a rejection of the idea of self-mastery.

Sometimes it really feels like it was another person who did something to us, or did not do something for us, that caused our suffering. In truth this is merely a false perception. It is a denial of our own authority and ability to determine our inner wellness. Plus, when we look at our past experiences from this extremely accountable view, we can usually see where our choices have led us to a certain path or outcome, regardless of how another person may have been involved.

Of course, the other person made their own choices that determined their need for healing and growth. However, from our healthiest perspective, they simply played the role we needed in order to teach us our truth. Had we been more connected in power to our Authentic Self, we would have created a very different outcome. And this other person would likely not have entered the picture.

This is how incredibly powerful we are when present. We are not only able to create more positive conditions while in our power, but we are also able to avoid entirely the need to experience certain lessons through suffering. New experiences are being created around us all of the time. To the extent that we can successfully monitor our own expressions of energy, within our own minds and out into the world, we will effectively direct our life toward the higher Divine qualities we most desire.

Based upon our external experiences we can learn much about our level of enlightenment, or need for awakening. However, outside of our conscious control, we still have the potential for our soul's expression to bring an experience to our humanity. This can be a very powerful and necessary part of our life path. It may be bring a potent interaction with some person, or some other significant event that has the potential for great transformation.

For our part, on this enlightened path, we must utilize our present moment awareness to deal with the new arising situation from a place of love and peace. Your ego may send many signals of fear-based thoughts that could potentially separate you from your higher power. Depending upon the event, you can be misguided in directions that lead to unconsciousness and suffering.

For example, if you win the lottery (something which is outside of your control) you will likely be very happy. Yet many new choices will need to be made that could either enhance your love or fear. You would still be wise to be very attentive to your Higher Self in each present moment as you navigate your many options.

If instead, the event is a car accident that hurt you or someone you love, your experience would feel very different. You may think, "Well I did nothing to create or deserve this, so I am going to be pissed off indefinitely." However, since this is your new reality, you would be wise to move toward the energy of acceptance of what-is. There is always a causation and consequent benefit to our experiences, whether or not it is evident at the time. You do not need to be happy that this happened, yet moving into your Presence is always the best space in which to realize the greatest benefit.

Shifting to this higher perspective will afford the best opportunity for you to deal with this new reality from a position of strength and love in each present moment. Otherwise, to abide in denial of, and resistance to what is, will only cause a furtherance of fearful (non-loving) choices which delay your wellness on all levels. This is the ego stance that wants to judge right or wrong from its selfish, limited understanding.

The examples above represent one of the great principles of enlightenment, and that is to be accountable for that which you control and accepting of that which is outside of your control. Instead of trying to control other people or outside circumstances, your efforts are toward monitoring your own energy and perceptions. You are seeking the highest ground from which to be most loving and empowered.

Do you not see this as a higher, healthier approach? Whether it has to do with the conditions of our original birth circumstances, or certain other significant events that happen during our life span, some things are beyond our human control and our ego's desires.

We can spend our lifetime whaling against something that we deem "unfair" or seemingly unbearable to our human condition, yet this serves no useful purpose. If we can effect a positive change going forward we should do it, if not, we accept it and move on. Enlightened living guides us to minimize a typically substantial amount of self-generated suffering.

You may now understand why this process of awakening and living more enlightened is supported by the realization of your Authentic Self. If your identity is merely human/ego, without the overlaying spiritual existence, everything that happens to our humanity takes on a greater significance. Our suffering, the injustices, the challenges, will all seem more devastating than they really are. This is how your ego always perceives things through its limited agenda.

When you know that you are a spiritual being having a human experience, you understand that how your humanity feels or thinks about any particular situation is temporary. It is just another experience. You will likely survive this, and continue on to have many more experiences. Not only that, on a higher level it is actually designed to teach and empower you. Then, when you can take the next step of being conscious in the present moment, you will claim the power to more easily transcend your human challenges.

Mastering your life involves striving to impact it based upon the positive flow of your energy and expressions. This will either have the power to change your circumstances to something more desirable to you, or it will give you the peace of understanding that will assist you in making the best of your circumstances. You are now shining the light of true power which comes from the higher principles related to your Authentic Self.

All of this is only possible when you can move out of a mindset that either holds you prisoner to past memories or relegates you to the perceived "hopelessness" of your future. Neither of these is real, they merely represent your habit of living in unconsciousness. They are distracting and disabling your power to connect with your truth. Do not invest your time and energy in this vortex of fear.

You must move into the present moment with a focus on acceptance of what is. And "what is" always entails that you are Spirit as well as human, you are bigger than the problems you perceive. At times this takes great faith in your truth, but this is choosing love over fear.

The love that you are is greater than the fear that you perceive. At all times you have a team of angels and spirit guides surrounding you with love, they are supporting and guiding you, but you have to listen. This listening for inspiration happens when you get present, peaceful, and open for their help.

I find that meditation is great for serving this process. Additionally, gratitude is very powerful for shifting your focus from your perceived problems toward a space of present receptivity and positivity. You must take the necessary actions to create the conditions of shifting your energy if you truly expect to create a better reality.

When you are present and connected to your Authentic Self you may best determine what choices or actions are appropriate for you in that moment. It is critically important to honor your truth. Release the pull of fear, guilt, shame, false expectations, the opinion of others, etc. Your unique life path is a constant stream of present moments for you to fulfill. Endeavor to experience this with wisdom and awareness.

Depending upon the energy of the surrounding experience you are dealing with, your truth may call for different actions. Sometimes your best choice is to choose to love yourself enough to accept that in this moment, "I just need to find some peace and feel what I feel." Not everything requires an immediate remedy. It is always best to deal with your emotions honestly, instead of withholding them until they build into something unhealthy.

True power comes from being aware of your higher truth connected to loving energy in the present moment. This supports you in making the most empowering choices that best honors your Authentic Self. These choices will bring the life lessons you need for healing, growth, and ascension, in the most satisfying manner.

CHAPTER 14

The Energy of Love

"When I was a child, I used to speak as a child, reason as a child; when I became a man, I did away with childish things. For now we see in a mirror dimly, but then face to face; now I know in part, but then I shall know fully just as I have been fully known. But now abide in faith, hope, love, these three; but the greatest of these is love."

- New Testament – 1 Corinthians 13: 11-13

The above quote from the Christian scriptures alludes to the energy and power of love. If you consider it more deeply, it is implying that we have a choice about the energy we choose, leading to true empowerment. This statement is coming from an enlightened perspective.

In 1 Corinthians, Paul is proclaiming the excellence of love, and that next to this most powerful quality all other things fall away. To me this quote also expresses perfectly that it is time for us to grow to be people who seek to live more enlightened, more loving. In a spiritual sense we have lived in the world as children, selfish and immature. Let us now shed our ignorance, claim the power of our Presence, and live a life of Mastery!

Through our life process we have been educated in many false teachings and accordingly have been stuck in the ego energy that has led to countless unsatisfying and challenging experiences. When we begin to recognize the light of our own truth we can understand that we do not have to continue repeating the painful lessons of our youth. Nor do we need to directly cause the suffering of others. We can know that it is not the things we possess, the prestige we garner, nor the human comforts we may enjoy that are most rewarding. The true highest experience of joy and fulfillment come from expressing and abiding in love.

What is this "love" that I am talking about? And why is this somewhat intimidating word for many people so significant? Unfortunately, we quite often have come to associate this word love with its opposite – which is fear. This is the ultimate ego-based delusion. And it stems from attaching fearful energy and meaning to the human consequences and actions around what we have considered human love.

Sometimes we think of love in terms of weakness or sentiment, but I am not using this word in a flowery Hallmark way, or as a substitute for assertive action and strength. Or we think of sex, commitment, and other romantic entanglements that have likely brought some form of suffering along the way. And finally, we may associate love with abandonment or other so-called "heart-breaking" circumstances.

However, I am referring to the "energy of love," which is the highest most powerful quality of energy. The expression and energy of love is the root quality for joy, peace, kindness, compassion, creativity, empowerment, faith, hope, gratitude, wellness, and enlightenment. It denotes a sincere unconditional caring and appreciation, and it is in alignment with the inner workings of the Source of all life.

True love is the internal recognition of your Divine Soul made manifest in the physical world.

The energy of love is expansive truth. This is the ruling principle of Universal Life Force; love always was and always will be. This energy runs independent and concurrent with all matter. And, as humans, it is our inner truth and strength when we choose to claim it.

You cannot have inner strength without loving yourself for your very being and nature. Most of us only "love" ourselves when we do something that others admire, and this is not love, but fear. Or we only "love" others when they do the things for us that we want done. We have made love conditional, yet the spiritual energy of love is unconditional. As you connect more often with your Authentic Self, the energy of love (Presence) will more easily be expressed outwardly in a supportive way toward others.

For the most part this powerful energy is operating outside of our limited mental perceptions. Much the way that we do not notice the Earth spinning at blinding speeds, this love energy or life force is always in play. It is up to us to connect our awareness to this potent force as often as possible.

As the energy representative of our Higher Self, love is naturally received and offered when we are conscious. Otherwise, when infected by the ego-mind, what we call love is contrived and self-serving. We may all recognize this within past "love" relationships. Love is a gift we accept from Spirit, and not something to be manufactured or controlled.

Love is not about romance, which is a human endeavor. It is energy to be shared with all beings, whether partner, family, friend, or stranger. And this is the significance of Unity Consciousness (to be discussed in Part III). We are each to offer our highest light and loving energy in all of our thoughts, words, and actions.

This higher energy is not promoted through the ego-based culture in which humanity functions. It requires that we awaken in order to realize our truth, and connect to higher consciousness. This is the path that leads to our healing, growth, and ascension.

Enlightened living is in alignment with the love energy within and around us. As we awaken to our own truth and develop greater awareness in the present moment, we will embody this Presence more strongly and consistently. Our attitudes and perceptions will shift, whereby we find greater purpose, meaning, compassion, and peace, within our daily lives. And we will create more opportunities to contribute our loving service to all others. There is no mastering your life without the energy of love.

CHAPTER 15

The Energy of Fear

"The only thing we have to fear, is fear itself"

- Franklin Delano Roosevelt

In truth, from the higher spiritual perspective of Oneness and the elimination of duality, there is only love. And the energy of fear is simply the perceived absence of the energy of love. However, for the sake of discussion and the teaching in a society that is largely disconnected from Spirit and therefore living within the delusion of fear, I am treating this as a force that must be overcome. While love is always available to us, we must continually and intentionally endeavor to connect or abide in that higher energy.

This opposing energetic force is called FEAR. **The energy of fear is restrictive delusion.** Every present moment becomes a choice to live in either the energy of love or fear. Regardless of our apparent human circumstances, we all came into this life with free will. It is our awareness in the present moment that offers the power to choose love. For without this power we naturally fall into the ego delusion of fear, and often believe that no other choice even exists.

A breakdown of President Roosevelt's famous quote tells you that fear does not exist in the absolute, and therefore it is a man-made illusion. It is a choice that becomes a self-fulfilling obstacle to true empowerment. When we choose fear we are blocking love. And in doing this we are blocking the Divine qualities for which we all aspire to experience (peace, joy, hope, wellness, etc.). In any specific moment these two energies are mutually exclusive, you are either abiding in love or in fear.

We typically bounce back and forth between these two energies depending upon our external stimulus and level of consciousness. In the light of our own highest power – Divine Presence - we choose love. The challenge is that from birth we are taught to fear virtually everything, and we then this unloving energy is reinforced repeatedly throughout our lives.

First let me explain what I am talking about when I use the word fear. We have simplistically learned to define this term to mean that we are afraid for our physical safety. But the energy of fear is much more pervasive and disempowering than that. *Fear is the overriding quality of every problem in the human world*. It manifests into such terms and conditions as anger, hate, greed, guilt, abuse, discrimination, insecurity, vanity, shame, ignorance, judgment, violence, poverty, envy, and lack of all kinds.

When I talk about elevating your consciousness in order to express the energy of love in all of your endeavors, this represents a very significant shift from how we have learned to experience the world. We all have been indoctrinated into a culture where the qualities of fear are perpetrated all around us. And anything that exists in the material world, exist energetically within us as well. This necessitates the need for us to identify with the higher truth of ourselves in order to create a new inner wellness and reality.

Some have described our fearful thoughts and actions as "sin," and the propensity to function in this way as our "sinful nature." However, my awareness finds this term to be based in fear, and therefore, not from Divinity, but from man. I prefer the term ego-nature. It is our ego that functions as our self-interest based in fear, whereas our true identity as Spirit only exists in the energy of love. This explains why our higher purpose is to realize our Authentic Self in order to connect to our true Presence.

The truth is that this human experience, as dark as it may seem at times, is part of an overall spiritual journey that we have chosen for purposes of our Soul's growth and evolution. Being born into sin sounds like a punishment or defect to me, which serves no real purpose in a loving Universe. I would prefer to say that in the relatively brief history of mankind we have primarily chosen to attach our energetic identity to ego, which focuses on the self-preservation of our temporary human life. And without a sufficient connection to Divine love, fear takes over and causes all manner of human suffering.

The predominant thinking has been that this physical life is all there is, and if I don't do everything I can to protect myself (from others and lack), then I will suffer and die. This mindset separates us from the energy of Divine love, and therefore by definition is fear inducing.

This majority point of view has over time created a collective consciousness (or should I say unconsciousness) steeped in the energy of fear. Yet, this energy of fear that we have accepted as our reality (as human nature) is actually a choice when we can shift to a more enlightened perspective. I hope that you are learning that Mastering your life and transforming in this way is ultimately a choice. It's one that has great significance toward the ascension and evolution of this world.

CHAPTER 16

Choosing Love over Fear

"I believe that every single event in life happens in an opportunity to choose love over fear."

- Oprah Winfrey

Thus far I have discussed the difference between the energies of love and fear. I have also instructed that the power to make the choice for love, or to live enlightened, occurs by being aware of this opportunity in each present moment. Let's talk more about what this really means for you in your everyday life.

When you choose to offer loving energy you are in alignment with your true higher power, and are then in a position to create favorable circumstances energetically for yourself and others. The bottom line is that you have a choice in how you experience and express your energy. But you can only effectively do this when conscious in the present moment.

Conversely when you express the energy of fear, you are in that moment cutoff from your power. You are functioning in a lower energetic vibration, focused on some facet of self-interest and disconnected from your loving truth. This often leads to the creation of consequences that are at best unsatisfying and potentially the causes of suffering. And obviously, this is less supportive of the wellness of other people as well.

With each choice we make we energetically impact both ourselves and others. This happens directly and indirectly, and in either subtle or more intense ways. We impact our lives directly, as evidenced by the consequences of our choices. And

115

we also indirectly affect the collective consciousness by the quality of the energy we exude. This reinforces the truth, that on the level of Spirit, we are all connected.

In the more subtle and routine instances, the expression of how we mentally talk to ourselves in each moment is a choice for love or fear. Most of our self-talk has come as a result of the lifelong ego-based input from others and the collective unconsciousness. When unobserved through mindfulness, we are not even aware of the damage we are creating with the negative thoughts we think.

We may have attached our energy to some self-judgment about a past personal "failure," embarrassment, disappointment, or feeling of lack in comparison to someone else. This now regularly plays in our head as doubt, insecurity, and resignation that stops us from fulfilling our purpose. It is blocking our expansive love energy, and therefore, we feel restricted and disempowered.

The first key is to use your awareness to notice this disturbance or depleted state. Next, you may apply higher wisdom to know that you have a choice to correct your false expressions and elevate to a higher energetic space. Most of the time our negative self-talk is habitual and unconscious. As soon as you become aware of this negativity, it is no longer buried in unconsciousness. You now are present, and you have an opportunity to choose thoughts that are more loving and compassionate.

It is important that you develop a connection to an identity of yourself as a person worthy of love and wellness on all levels. That is why "Realizing your Authentic Self" is taught first in this book on Self-Mastery. This is the wisdom that authorizes you to accept a higher purpose, potential, and accountability for your wellness. And this process of choosing love in each present moment is how we integrate the identity of our spiritual nature into our everyday human experiences.

When you are present with your thoughts you can notice whether they are loving or fearful. However, present or not, you are literally choosing to be empowered or disempowered in that moment. Your experiences will eventually manifest as the result of your expressions of energy and then you will need to deal with the consequences that follow. Better to be present and aware of your energy as you express it, to ensure the greater likelihood of more positive and satisfying experiences.

If you have an experience that created (through your thoughts) great internal suffering, you likely will have that fearful thought return often. This not only brings an element of misery in the moment, but impacts your choices going forward. But with your awareness you can correct your thinking in present time, and re-align to your truth.

First, shift to thoughts about compassion and forgiveness for yourself. Honor your past experience merely as a life lesson. You are not denying it happened, so there is no self-deception involved. However, you are intentionally detaching from the energy of this past experience since you are now living in the present. This is always the higher truth and the energy of love.

Next, know that no matter what the fear is telling you, you have a clean slate in the present to create something better. This is likely not an instant manifestation, yet it is a shifting of your energy which leads to your healing, growth, and well-being. This is choosing self-love, and is the realization of your higher nature. Eventually you will claim a level of power over that past false belief to where it will likely just fade away into the nothingness that it actually is.

Notice that this is only the damage that we do to ourselves; we are creating this suffering all on our own, even if our ego mind tries to hold someone else to blame. The truth is, regardless of our fear and delusion we are the only ones who can create our suffering. And unfortunately, we have become quite skilled in this behavior.

Let's take an example where we feel that someone else hurt or disrespected us. Maybe someone influential in your life told you that you were not good enough to do something you really had a passion to do. Or maybe another person called you lazy, stupid, worthless, or used some other damaging and false label. One more example would be, if at some point in your life someone betrayed your trust, manipulated or mistreated you in a significant way to your detriment. Everyone who has lived enough human life has experienced one or all of these types of energetic attacks from other people. And when we take in this energy from a place of unconsciousness, it can be quite disabling.

You will likely internalize this negativity differently based upon your inner power and connection to self-love. However, these are examples of how the expression of energy can have a devastating effect upon us. Incidentally, not only have we all received this energy, but we also have each expressed this toxicity to others as well.

Whether this happened when you were a child or last week, you very likely may still have that poison living inside you and affecting you negatively today. The first step to healing this energy is always to get present as these thoughts arise and notice the feeling of disempowerment. If there has been an event that is so powerful that it routinely causes fear and anxiety then you will want to address this healing proactively. This is addressed in detail in Chapter 17.

Benefits of Choosing Love

Modern day example: I am the CEO of the company; therefore, (in my ego-based beliefs) I am worthy of living in lavish wealth, while many hardworking employees must make do on substandard wages and conditions in order to serve me and the shareholders. Though I will make speeches about "caring and teamwork," privately I feel justified in accepting the great disparity in power and compensation. Eventually this will bring down the company and many workers will lose their jobs, regardless, I am getting mine while I can.

Within a greater connection to the energy of love, the CEO/Management would consider the value of all who are connected and contributing to the ongoing success of the company. This is the new Conscious Business model. The leaders in our organizations must be the first to bring a higher energy for the good of all; they set the tone for the rest.

As opposed to merely giving lip service, a true leader understands their responsibility to lead, serve, and support those in their charge. Greater success will always be realized when all members feel that they are valued for their contributions, as they will be more connected to the outcome of the quality of their labor. In elevating one member, we lift the whole team.

Often times, we don't recognize that we ourselves are making a life of choosing fear-based objectives. But the truth is that in some big or small way (as you may define it) we all abide in fear until we consciously and intentionally choose love. It is time to make it a greater priority to elevate our definition of "integrity" to include the energy of love. In all of our choices we must realize that in addition to our own well-being we have an obligation to consider the well-being of others.

The energy of love plays into our humanity on many occasions and in many forms when we choose to embody our Authentic Self. Just as true, the energy of fear manifests in the behaviors and conditions of mankind that have created so much suffering. However, even if you are a skeptic concerning anything spiritual, I ask you to take this journey with me. My intention is to support how the utilization of this higher perspective is beneficial in making more empowering choices leading to enhanced human experiences.

As we shed light on the aspect of our being that is Spirit, we can shift into a higher perspective of our human lives and the fulfillment of our greater potential. We can begin to realize that many of our needs are supported by an inner awareness, power, and accountability, which then reduce our desire to harm others. And we are less inclined to define our value and significance according to external qualities.

If we can begin to abide in a more loving and peaceful state within ourselves, we cease to be consumed with filling this otherwise vacant cavity by requiring other people to "love" us, respect us, support us, approve and validate us. This applies in a very practical way to enhancing our self-image, personal relationships, careers/contributions, health, etc. And by the very nature of elevating our own well-being independent of the energy or resources of others, we add to the collective welfare of all.

Mastering your life involves knowing that love is a choice, and is the recognition and alignment of the Divine energy that is always a part of you. You then endeavor to live within this higher present moment space as your ongoing priority. This is not an intellectual decision to suddenly be more loving to others, while at the same time being bound by your own fear (in all of its masks). That approach is not sustainable, and it is ineffective when endeavoring to love all beings equally.

If you can accept that this world of fear has not produced the qualities of life that are most beneficial to yourself and all other people, then you are at a good starting point for understanding the significance of living in your true power as an enlightened human. Learn to release the old ego identity, in favor of your more encompassing and loving Authentic Self, and then make it your moment-to-moment intention and practice to choose love over fear.

Examples of Choosing Love over Fear

#1 - You are driving your car in a safe manner and speed; let's say a couple miles per hour (5 or less) over the posted speed limit. Someone races up behind you and it feels like they are sitting on your rear bumper, and maybe they are even making "I'm annoyed" gestures. For me, this has always disturbed my peace, and in the past (while more unconscious) I might have tensed up and expressed my displeasure in a rude way. But I have learned that this is an example of an excellent opportunity to choose love over fear; this is a spiritual lesson for me (and maybe you too).

I cannot change their behavior; I can only change my perception of the situation. If I continue to watch them in the rear view mirror, I tend to get and stay angry (even beyond the incident). This is because my ego is saying, "that person is a jerk, they are infringing upon my safety, and I feel threatened and pissed off." This is an example of choosing fear (judgment, anger, and anxiety).

Or, I can double-check my speed, and if I am satisfied with it, choose to be content that, in reality, I am fine. I can then remind myself that what they do is for them and not for me to be concerned about (it is not like they are shooting at me, a very different reality). In fact they may have their own legitimate reasons for speeding. I may focus on the road ahead and maintain a positive present moment mental focus – I am now in my power. They will likely just pass me at some point, no harm done.

This is choosing the energy of love (compassion, peace, allowance of what is). You can see that the choice for love is based on the true reality of the situation. And the choice for fear is based upon what my over-active anxiety for self-interest is telling me. Ego is interrupting my power with chatter about the negative "what if." And this happens often throughout your day.

You can see how road rage occurs between two unconscious individuals, both controlled by ego and fear, a potentially disastrous outcome for no good reason. Again, if reality changes in a way that requires action, then you will deal with it appropriately; we are never to evade responsibility for our own wellness.

#2 - Let's say that you recently started dating someone, and in the course of getting to know this person they express themselves in ways (maybe subtle at first) that raise a few red flags. For example, some of their expressions feel controlling and critical of you (without cause). But you are attracted to some of their qualities (physical features or otherwise), and on that level it feels good to be around them.

Still, you can't help but feel that there is some disconnect and that this person is not accepting you as you are, nor do they seem to have your best interest at heart. If you are paying attention to your intuition (higher awareness), you will clearly sense this warning on an energetic level. But when controlled by the fear embedded in your mind, you may likely discount the higher truth that is being offered through your Spirit.

We then may try to rationalize all of the reasons why it could work if we gave it a chance. You think, "I really like these certain things about her/him, and these other things I can help change. And as far as their tendency to judge and accuse me of things that are untrue, they just need to get to know me better. Plus, it is really a pain to start over and try to find someone else." Isn't this something we all have done?

First of all, never go into a relationship aware of significant problems, but thinking that you are going to change or "fix" someone. You are simply asking the Universe for a lesson in suffering. This is the classic co-dependent situation. We may convince ourselves that trying to "be there for them" is admirable, but in truth, when it dishonors us, it is just a way of choosing fear over love. If we loved ourselves enough to know that we deserve better, we would not pick someone that needs our "fixing".

So, depending upon your need for inner healing in this area, you will make your choice to either continue or end the relationship. The deeper choice is to either choose to honor your loving truth or follow your inner fear-based motivations. And of course, the appropriate consequences will play out as a life lesson. This is an example of how we create our path, and why it is invalid to blame others for our suffering.

When living in mastery, you will honor your own true knowing and make the choices that are most supportive to your well-being. There is a very critical choice for love or fear that you are required to make here. This is part of the higher value in attracting this particular person. And this is all about you at this point. Ask yourself: Are you going to listen to Spirit or ego?

A choice for love means that you are going to hold to your highest value and inner strength, regardless of what another person may say or do to persuade or manipulate you. A choice for fear means that you are going to disregard your true sense and hope that one or both of you will change in the future to make this relationship mutually supportive and loving. Incidentally, if they are not right for you, you are not the best fit for them either. But through fear we sometimes make choices to "not hurt" the other person, which is just a way of abdicating our responsibility to our self and others.

Always choose to love yourself (in the Spirit sense) first, or face the much more difficult lesson of dishonoring your truth and choosing fear which always ends in suffering. By the way, in choosing to honor your inner knowing you not only spare yourself much pain and grief, but you align with your higher love energy. You are now in a better position to attract a more positively compatible match.

Most relationships are co-dependent to some extent because we are always dealing with some form of ego. And when primarily controlled by ego, you will attract a very powerful relationship partner to teach you to be more accountable for your own love and wellness. I know this because I have chosen to learn from such experiences many times. But as I have been able to understand my past choices and shift my energy toward greater consciousness, I am now empowered to honor intuition and choose love. This is an example of awakening to Enlightened Living.

#3 - You are at work doing your job, when an irate customer contacts you. They are upset that an order was not delivered as promised to them by your company. You did your job the best you could, but conditions arose that necessitated the delay of delivery. This has put you and your contact in a challenging position. Therefore, you are getting berated by this person who is feeling their own stress.

How are you going to handle this situation where you know it is not your fault personally, yet you are being angrily challenged as a representative of your company? Of course the goal is to figure out how you are going to satisfy this customer and keep their business. But apart from that you have a choice to connect with the energy of love or attach to fear. This will directly affect your expressions to your customer, and the tone of the situation.

In the end this is not only a business problem, it is also a personal empowerment issue. Regardless of what was going on before you received this telephone call (or visit), you must get present quickly. If based on the caller's challenges you choose fear, you may feel overly personally attacked. Your ego is going want to judge "right and wrong" in the view of self-preservation, which may end up in a name-calling debacle and no one wins.

If you can set aside their aggression and choose love in this instance, you may accept that their words are only reflective of their stress in the moment. They are not an accurate depiction of you personally. Then with much greater calm you can find compassion for their predicament. This is what they are really wanting, even if they are aggressively expressing fear (anger). You may now begin to discuss potential solutions, if any, to the business problem. However, you can and should abide in the inner strength that will express an unwillingness to receive verbal abuse from this person.

The choice for love is an acknowledgement that they are merely expressing fear and looking for support, and you will try to assist with that. Your choice for fear is based in the imagined scenario that this is about you being personally attacked and that it is wrong for them to treat you this way. In fear you are not interested in solving the problem, just in presenting a positive image of yourself. Therefore, choosing love opens the door to new opportunities for growth and healing, while choosing fear does not resolve anything and creates additional problems.

I am not saying that this is easy. We have been raised to defend ourselves first and foremost. And to allow someone to "abuse or attack" us is considered weak. What I am suggesting is to bring in the awareness of what is reality and what is illusion. Have the inner strength to feel secure within your being when someone is merely expressing their ego energy (their fear) around or toward you. You are not required to participate in the same lower energy, you always have a choice.

#4 - One more example of an opportunity to choose love over fear occurs within your own mind, possibly on a fairly regular basis. Our self-talk is very powerful, and will either create new blessings or further cause our suffering; hence we must be more conscious of what we tell ourselves. When you make a mistake, or if you tried something that did not work out as well as you hoped, you have a choice to make. And this could be something recent or many years ago. If you tell yourself, "I am such a loser" or "I am terrible at this," you have chosen fear. In this case you are declaring to the Universe (your higher power) that you ARE a loser, you ARE terrible, and essentially unworthy or incapable of doing or being something you desire.

In truth, you are simply giving in to your fear in this moment of false perception. You are likely not intending to attach yourself to these negative proclamations for now and all times. Often this is an unconscious ingrained habit for many people. Elevate your present moment awareness and do not continue to create the energetic cause that may manifest experiences that support your false claim.

If something did not work out the way you wanted, you can admit that. But then tell yourself that this was part of the learning process and declare, "I am fully capable of improving and doing this better in the future." By choosing love you are planting seeds for future success; by choosing fear you are closing the door to opportunities and prolonging needless suffering. Always use the powerful "I am" statement in positive ways.

You can see that the opportunity to choose love or fear, Spirit or ego, is presented to us in two typical and routine scenarios: First, in confrontational situations with other people. And this actually reflects the true higher purpose of relationships. They are to facilitate the exchange of energy, either for purposes of support or lessons leading to healing and growth. The second scenario takes place within us when being confronted with self-judgment, undesirable memories of the past, or anxiety about the future.

Dealing with these experiences can feel quite challenging, especially with a limited view of your true power. However, this is the process of growth and development within the human involvement that supports the fulfillment of the Soul's purpose. Your experiences are created by you to facilitate your evolution. Free will dictates that the choice of whether you live in love or fear is yours alone.

There is no enlightened living without awareness and accountability in the present moment.

When we make a mistake and choose fear in any situation, either through ignorance or a lack of discipline, it is our higher awareness that will notice the impact this has on our energy. You can learn to "tune in" to this subtle (and sometimes not-so-subtle) system that governs your energy body. You may notice when your energy is stuck or you experience some form of anxiety. Or you can recognize when things are flowing in a more natural easy way. This is an internal barometer, and not merely the result of external circumstances.

Awareness of our energy is a great tool for self-assessment. Learn to sense the quality of your energy and allow it to guide your actions. Beyond the consideration of choices for love or fear, you can also gauge when to rest or exert your energy. This is a great tool for maintaining and optimizing physical wellness, and increasing effectiveness in your production.

Beyond the awareness that such things are possible, a key ingredient is patience and trust in your higher nature. These are all advantages that you will miss if you are simply racing through your life trying to "check all of the boxes" that the world has defined for you. The greater your intention toward living your life in such an enlightened state, the more successful you will be in the management of your energy. And it is your energy that is ultimately creating your present and future experiences, and therefore, the joy and fulfillment you hope to attain.

Choosing love in any present-moment situation is a choice to align with Spirit, which is your highest natural state. This is not some out-of-body, over-the-top religious experience.

It is simply an advantageous position from which to make empowering choices that aid your development and the quality of your human experiences.

I like to refer to this as, "more conscious living" (which is the subtitle of my first book), because it requires a higher degree of intention, mindfulness, and discipline. Apart from this level of consciousness you will habitually choose the preference of your ego, which is connected to fear. This is why an essential key to Enlightened Living is to claim your power by choosing love in the present moment.

CHAPTER 17
Seven Steps for Shifting from Fear to Love

"There are two primary choices in life: to accept conditions as they exist, or accept the responsibility for changing them."

- Denis Waitley

Here are some steps that will lead you to choose love when dealing with situations that seem to have brought much suffering. With the full understanding of the power that always exists within you due to your unconditionally loving Spirit nature, you can begin to truly dissect your experiences and ascend to your true higher reality.

1) **Connect to your Authentic Self.** Do this by becoming aware of yourself on a level beyond your mind, body, and disempowering false beliefs. This may best be facilitated within a meditation practice. Shift your awareness to become the noticer of your being. Feel a sense of separation from your fear, at least for these few moments of spiritual practice. Identifying with your Authentic Self shifts you into your true reality and invites the higher energy of love to this process of healing.

2) **Realize and accept that you have chosen to attach to the energy of fear that has left you powerless and separated from love regarding this issue.** For whatever else you have experienced, within this situation you have identified yourself as a victim. And you now desire to transcend this false identity. You have unwittingly handed the power of your own loving energy over to the delusion of your fear. Acknowledge that this is true.

Now you have the awareness of truth that will support you in reclaiming your power, and assist in your opening to receive the higher lesson of the experience. If your energy matches any of the forms of fear (listed in Chapter 15), then this is the proof that you chose fear instead of love in this instance. Now, having accepted this truth, your awareness and intentions can help you shift your outlook and energy toward thoughts and actions that support healing, growth, and evolution.

3) **Connect with the awareness of compassion and forgiveness for yourself.** Your past experience, which brought the energy of fear, was a life experience that you attracted in order to learn your own higher truth and value. When we honor ourselves we naturally choose love, and when we don't we are given the opportunity to feel the effects of our self-abandonment through fear and suffering. You did not understand previously that you had a choice, but now that you know, offer the power of forgiveness to yourself and know that in the present you are reclaiming your truth by choosing love.

4) **In your meditative internal space, ask to see clearly the value of the experience or situation, leading you to greater love, growth, and healing.** With an enlightened realization of the truth of the experience, unattached to fear, you may now uncover the inner beliefs that led you to the choices you made. In this more detached space there is no present suffering or delusion. You can see that you attracted this as an opportunity to learn about certain aspects of your energetic life that are in need of healing. This pertains to both the original situation and the ongoing thoughts about that event.

Beginning with full accountability, guidance will come in the form of peaceful thoughts and feelings, which give clarity and purpose to the event or situation. The wisdom that you receive is coming from your Higher Self. It is shining the light of truth which awakens you to the power of love that may transform you from your fear. This "shining the light of love" onto your path is the very definition of enlightenment. The healing takes place as you are able to replace your fearful energy around the perceived problem with love.

5) **Now that you are receiving the power of love within, take steps to express this energy outward.** If there are lingering circumstances that require your attention and resolution, you will of course be obligated to take appropriate action. However, you may now do this in a way that is accountable to Spirit, and not attached to ego. You may have a greater inner strength and understanding that now supports you in dealing with situations that previously held you captive to fear.

Now, within the full light of truth, open your heart to feel the energy of forgiveness for any others involved. This need not necessarily be expressed to them. The primary purpose is to release the negative energy that you have been holding. Energetically this release supports them as well, though they may not be aware of it. Remember, the only healing you have authority over is your own.

The other person is responsible for their life lessons, growth, and healing. This is part of their journey toward enlightenment, which is up to them to realize. Since you are accountable for your energy, you are the only person who could internalize their remarks or actions in a way that brought suffering to you. Just as only you can correct this error and reclaim your power by choosing love. Incidentally, being spiteful and holding a grudge against this person reflects your choice for fear and not love, and will only continue to poison your life.

6) **The final step is to accept this sacred moment of transformation and healing by giving thanks and gratitude to the Divinity within and surrounding you.** You have received the true value of healing and growth from an experience that once brought fear and suffering. You have energetically offered forgiveness to yourself and all others involved. And you have realized, through full accountability, your inner power for choosing love over fear. This all occurred as a result of shifting your perception from being a victim to claiming your present-moment power. You regained higher consciousness.

This is truly powerful! And it can and must be applied to any situation that has left you disempowered and unsatisfied. Your objective is to fill the negative fearful space within your Being (mind, body, spirit) with the energy of love. You had simply allowed darkness to creep into your human experience, but then through your higher awareness you have shone the light of truth upon the ego-induced situation. You have awakened to live more enlightened. This is the connection to your Authentic Self that allows you to transcend ego challenges.

7) **Repeat as needed.** Often this inner work will release your fear and facilitate your healing in any given situation permanently. It is always more about your connection to your Authentic Self than any particular experience. However, while you are still realizing and integrating your true higher nature, you may find that you once again choose to attach to fear relative to the experiences that have had a more profound impact on your life. Transcending this experience may be an ongoing practice, which likely will be less intensive each time it happens.

In any case you are healing on a deeper level, and therefore, you must continue to choose love for yourself surrounding this situation. Maintain a powerful faith in your connection to Divinity which supports you in your healing. Stick with it because eventually it too will fade away and your light will have obliterated this particular darkness.

This is the internal process of choosing love over fear that is transformational. Having released this negativity which was blocking your true power you now open to opportunities for the expansion of light (or enlightenment). Depending upon the specifics of the experience you are free to connect to your power and move forward without being blocked by your fear.

The process described above is valid for any past situation in which you felt diminished by the thoughts, words, or actions of another toward you. Always remember that you are not requiring or expecting any particular action or shift from the other person. In the energy of love, we heal our self and accept others as they are. Your healing is simply you re-aligning with your truth.

In a similar way, this process is critical for retrieving your power from situations where you unconsciously added to the potential for suffering of another by your expressions of negatively-charged energy. We are always accountable for our own inner healing and for the energy that we express toward others. In this case your ongoing fear may manifest as guilt or shame.

However, since you only have the power of the present, you cannot undo or take back anything from the past. Therefore, fulfill the inner healing process for shifting your energy to love, and gain the awareness of your energetic expressions in order to move forward with greater love for others. If reasonable and appropriate, you may make amends to the aggrieved party.

PART II: Exercises

1) Practice tuning in to your present-moment awareness. In addition to your meditation practice, make a general mental note of how often you can notice yourself in the present moment versus how often you get lost in thoughts of the past or future.

2) As you become more mindful and present, take notice of your energy. Are you connected to love and feeling empowered to express peace, joy, contentment, gratitude, kindness, greater mental focus, etc.? Or are you attached to fear and feeling general disempowerment in the form of anxiety, anger, dissatisfaction, resentment, judgment, lack of focus, etc.? The mere fact that you are able to notice your awareness is evidence of your higher identity. From this place you now may shift from fear to love.

3) Find at least one significant event or experience from your past that has continued to hold you in fear and suffering. Work through the steps listed in Chapter 17. After doing this, do you feel more connected to your truth and loving energy? Or are you still stuck in ego delusion? Continue to work through this process until you can fully accept this situation or experience as a blessing leading to inner healing and growth.

PART II: Affirmations

I AM empowered to choose Love.

I AM abiding in the energy of Love.

I AM Divine Love.

I AM grateful for my Love and Truth.

I AM my Highest Awareness.

I AM a powerful Spiritual Being.

I AM filled with Love for myself and others.

I AM living in Higher Consciousness.

I AM living in the present moment.

I AM now honoring my higher truth.

I AM now choosing Love and Wellness.

PART III:

EMBRACING UNITY CONSCIOUSNESS

"Whatever books you may read, you cannot realize the Divine merely by intellectual effort. One must put it into practice. That sense of oneness can only be promoted by the practice of love and not by any other means."

- Sri Sathya Sai Baba

PART III: Prologue

You may or may not be familiar with the term "Unity Consciousness." Let me tell you what I am referring to and why it is such a critical aspect for Mastering your Life. As we are able to accept and realize our own higher identity and value, we may claim greater empowerment in each present moment. This, then, becomes reflected in the manner in which we express our energy to all.

Embracing Unity Consciousness is the expression of Divine loving energy for and among all beings. This is the Oneness that moves us beyond the duality of good/bad, us/them, and me/you. Through our acceptance of our higher nature we have awakened to our Authentic Self. This guides us to an active perception and knowing that we and all humans are Divine, and therefore, part of the overall Universal Divinity. We are equal, no one is lesser or greater than anyone else.

Embracing Unity Consciousness is the greatest evidence of our own level of wellness and enlightenment. It is the practical application of our Divine Nature within our humanity. And it is the cultivation of our own inner healing, growth, and evolution.

Remember, enlightened living is supportive of both our spirituality and our humanity. And this is pertinent in the collective sense as well as our individual well-being. Without developing Unity Consciousness, life goes on as it has, pitting humans against humans for ego control. This is not only disempowering, but ultimately detrimental to all. Therefore, continue to elevate your consciousness to honor all people regardless of their perceived human differences.

PART III: Energetic Quality or Tool

I find that the Divine Energetic Quality or Tool that supports the Embracing of Unity Consciousness is our *ALLOWING or ALLOWANCE*. Even within our own healing transformation we understand that the subtle power of allowing leads to greater acceptance, compassion, and unconditional love. In the case of Unity, we are to simply allow that which is of our higher nature to exist among, and for, all beings. This represents a significant shift for humankind.

We are shifting toward enlightened living, but thanks to our lifelong ego training, we will be reminded of our fear quite often, especially in relation to other people. We must continue to progress to greater unconditional love for ourselves and all others. We must allow other people to live their path according to their level of consciousness, which will always be different than ours. And not only tolerate them, but offer our loving support and service as well.

The Divine energy of Allowing is very challenging to us, where the opposite energy of *JUDGEMENT* is most entrenched. Within our egocentric mindset, we want to be "right" within our separateness. Since we falsely judge our value against our perceptions of others, we try to elevate ourselves by judging them as "wrong." Yet in truth, it is an illusion that can only be eradicated by Unity Consciousness.

When we are more secure within our own self-love, we are accountable for ourselves, and we want to honor and serve others, not judge, condemn, or change them. The way in which we treat another is an indication of our own level of wellness and consciousness. Our highest understanding knows we are united in Spirt, regardless of our perceived differences.

CHAPTER 18
Are we really all that Different?

"I do believe that the original sources of all religions should be taught, because with that we will find our similarities, and not just our differences. I believe that if Mohammed, Buddha, Jesus, and Moses all got together they would be best friends because the spiritual basis of all religions is something that builds unity."

- Yehuda Berg

An Historical View of Separateness

Each of us has chosen to come into this human experience for our own purposes of growth, evolution, and service. In truth we are the Divine individuation of the Source of all that is. On a Soul level, this is what makes us the "individuals" responsible for our own life path. We recognize our separate physical bodies, personalities, qualities, and characteristics as the instruments we have chosen to assist us in participating in this human experience. This gives us the separation that we perceive from others.

Regardless of our appearance or ranking, we all share our origin and higher nature. Yet, for the sake of our human survival we have established a clear agenda of prioritizing our own well-being versus that of all others.

While here on Earth, we have chosen to experience our lives in groups of similarly self-identified people. You are part of a specific family, community, race, nationality, etc., not to mention gender characteristics and associated expectations.

143

You have been "educated" and inundated with an identification and belief system that sets you apart from other individuals and groups.

Historically this has provided a form of comfort to our egos. Our sense of safety and security seems enhanced by the perceived familiarity as opposed to the unknown. After all, if we can agree as a group that we are right and just, then we can feel better about ourselves and our circumstances. We then tend to justify any judgement or mistreatment of another group when we believe that it benefits us.

Whether street gang, country, race, or religion, we will trust and support our kind before someone from another group. And if we find some amount of security within our associations, conversely, we attach expressions of fear toward those outside of our group or classification.

In order to overcome our perceived limitations and lack of resources for adequate survival, we have learned to focus almost exclusively on our own selfish desires. We have abandoned our higher nature in favor of our ego identification. We have chosen fear over love.

We create rules, espouse beliefs, and engage behaviors that further support our separation and even act as justification for harming and eliminating opposing views. This is the ego-mind thought process originating in the clan mentality that we have continued up to this point in history.

So now the world has grown and advanced to include many different ideas, viewpoints, segments, and factions. And due to technology and other factors, we are more interconnected than ever before. Yet, instead of creating more unity, it seems as though we are holding as tight as ever to separation.

As with all human growth and evolution we have many people who are all too comfortable remaining in the "way things used to be." Of course, this is because they perceive the past as good to them and their "kind," and they do not want to lose their advantages. This automatically elicits a battle with those who have been oppressed in the past.

Evolution requires change, progress, and ascension in consciousness. This growth is first experienced as vulnerability, which the ego detests. Our ego's comfort holds us to our inherent fear, and as I said in Chapter 15, fear is restrictive delusion. Therefore, our human nature encourages us to resist change and continue this unenlightened mindset, even as we witness injustice and inequality all around us.

A great shift in consciousness is required for the sake of greater wellness for all. This is about realizing our true identity and more often choosing unconditional love over fear. This is not an easy proposition in a world controlled by ego. This will typically feel like sacrifice to those who are thriving in the world and fully attached to their comforts and position. They say that freedom is not free, well neither is equality.

Interestingly enough, the people who control the most wealth and power seem to be more acutely controlled by fear. They are identifying themselves according to ego, and therefore believe that they have the most to lose. In truth, they may have the most to give and gain, if only their mindset was on love and not fear.

Much of the world is desperate for change. Many humans have been repressed and marginalized in our society. Clearly they never benefited from the "good old days."

Hence, the battle of evolution wages on. It is not a matter of *if*, but *when* the current power is displaced for the betterment of the masses. Without the awakening and shifting toward Unity Consciousness, this transition will be very costly and painful. This, of course, would be unfortunate for all.

Yet, all of this is due to our ego-control and false perceptions. Our differences need not cause hate, wars, famines, poverty, and injustice. Until we can view ourselves from a higher identity we will be powerless to make much progress toward equality and wellness for all people. We must all be able to look beyond our own self-interest to understand the ways in which we benefit most by supporting each other as humans.

How we are Similar as Humans

Are we really that different? Even putting aside our shared higher nature for a minute and looking exclusively at our human qualities, it's a fact that all people need the same things to survive and thrive. Don't we all desire to be connected to others in the energy of love? Don't we all need the necessary supplies of healthy food, clean water and air, access to medicine and health care? Don't we each need a basic standard of a home to live in? And don't we each desire to be safe from violence and crime?

We also each need an opportunity to learn in a system of education that helps to develop both life skills and technical skills which can be offered in service to others. Our technology should be working to help provide the desires and necessities described above. Instead, it seems it is primarily adding to the comforts of a few, or eliminating employment opportunities for the many (for the sake of profit). Are we working toward real solutions to human problems, or just creating more gadgets to entertain and distract us?

Without meeting their basic needs, no person could experience their best opportunity for a happy, healthy, and successful life. We have a choice to accept and honor the value of all people, and this encourages greater participation and contribution from all. From here we create peace and Unity.

Disadvantaged does not mean defective;
Advantaged does not mean superior.

CHAPTER 19

The Need for Unity Consciousness

"If you see yourself in others, who could you harm?

- Buddha

Clearly, from the standpoint of our basic human needs and desires, we are all quite similar. Then, why do we judge other humans as so different? And why do we see them as unworthy of the same qualities that we expect for ourselves? Why is someone with a certain skin color, gender, nationality, or religion better or worse than anyone else?

Are some people entitled with a superior birthright? Ordained so by God or kings? From the higher view of our Divine Nature and Unity Consciousness this makes no sense. It is pure ego-based delusion – with its origins in fear and control. Or do we need more wars, death, and suffering to teach us this truth?

This is why we must awaken to our true identity, which is shared by all people. Everything written in the previous chapters of this book have led to support this higher treatment of ourselves and our fellow humans/Souls on Earth. Our false ego identification is killing and harming millions of people. And it does not need to be this way.

Of course, it is not acceptable for any person or group to be justified in committing violence upon another. And we must have rules that help to encourage safety for all people. Yet, every human problem (including violence) comes from false ego identification. It all comes from fear.

Until those who consider themselves "righteous," awaken to express loving energy to all beings, they have no authority to condemn other people. And if they really were righteous they would have no desire to do so. In the name of "self-protection of our way of life," humans are justifying the commitment of all manner of atrocities. We must begin to transcend this delusion. We are to observe our human challenges from a higher perspective if we want to solve them in a way that promotes peace, Unity, and evolution.

The real problem has been that we have been unwilling to take this higher approach, and not that we are incapable of peaceful resolutions. We must be much more willing to remove the log from our own eye, as opposed to destroying someone else for the speck in theirs. We may think that we are better than another person (or nation), and if this is true, it is only by degrees.

If we don't start focusing on our own ability and responsibility for healing our own issues, and then honoring all others equally, we won't effectively improve the human condition. We will simply burden future generations with a world increasingly filled with fear and hate - not to mention a planet that may become unsuitable for human habitation.

Our principal attitude has been that as long as "my group and I" are doing okay, I am not going care about finding solutions for the suffering of other people. Does this sum up human history and unconsciousness? This astonishingly selfish, unenlightened, and inhumane way of thinking and behaving is still rampant today throughout the world. Could there possibly be a better time for us to awaken to live more enlightened?

If we were to focus on our similarities, as spiritual beings having a human experience, we would look upon each other as brothers and not threats (rivals or enemies). Clearly, from where we are today, this is a transition of significant proportion because there are many people attached and predisposed to their old biases (fears).

Therefore, we start by recognizing that we are all equal and worthy within our higher natures. And then we may gradually reduce any validity of focusing on a perceived devaluation of anyone based upon our differences. Evolution is slow and steady.

The first way to do this is to begin to become the masters of our own higher truth and see *ourselves* differently. We need to eliminate the fear and judgment within us before we can express love outwardly to all others. The process of enlightened living leads us to this very thing. Even while attending to our physical needs we can still begin to identify ourselves as spiritual beings on our Soul journey.

Self-Realization is connecting to your higher nature, in the fulfillment of your highest goals. There are no "enlightened" goals that involve judging, demeaning, or mistreating any other human/Soul! Accept your responsibility for balancing out your ego energy with the integration of your Divine loving energy. We are Master's created in love, and not sinners relegated to fear. We must realize our higher mission and identification as it relates to our humanity. And we all share this purpose and potentiality.

Through practice we can take this to the practical level of improving our awareness of what is really happening within our experiences and interactions. This will now show us the truth of what we are expressing in our thoughts, feelings, words, and actions. And we may elevate the view of our lives as empowered, and therefore, fully accountable for our expressions and reactions to and among other people.

We more easily maintain our inner strength and stay on purpose even when we appear to be unsupported by others. We understand that we can more effectively elevate the consciousness in the world by living enlightened rather than by judging and condemning others. In truth, when living this way, we are rarely harmed by other people.

In accord with our own inner development we are now more willing to accept the ways in which other people live differently than we do. While we are practicing healthy habits and taking responsibility for our own wellness, we recognize two things. One, I don't "need" you to act in a way that makes me feel better about myself. Therefore, I am not offended when you don't. And two, since I am stronger within a connection to my higher identity, I am now more willing to share my unconditional loving energy and resources in support of you.

When I talked about choosing love over fear, this is what I meant as it relates to Unity Consciousness. Do I choose fear and notice all the ways in which you are different, and therefore, threatening to me (in my ego delusion)? Or, do I choose to recognize the higher spiritual love and value in each of us? Knowing that I am worthy and capable of my own well-being, I may now overcome the tendency to judge and fear you.

This process of awakening to Enlightened Living and Mastering your Life involves a change in your mindset, perceptions, practices, and habits. In truth, when you can begin to evolve in this way, your reality will shift. The same person you previously saw as a rival or a problem can now be recognized as just another spiritual being on their own unique path and journey. If enough people change their reality from fear to love, then the experience of this world will evolve for all.

CHAPTER 20
Promoting Unity and Equality

"All are caught in an inescapable network of mutuality, tied in a single garment of destiny. Whatever affects one directly, affects all indirectly. I can never be what I ought to be until you are what you ought to be, and you can never be what you ought to be until I am what I ought to be."

- Martin Luther King Jr.

Along with the inner healing and transformation that elevates the quality of your life, the principles of enlightenment encourage you to outwardly express Unity Consciousness. This is a progression in higher awareness that requires great intention followed by consistent practice. The purpose of your practice is to transcend the fear-based cultural indoctrination that taught you to judge yourself as good-bad-different.

As we routinely judge ourselves according to our perception of ego merit, we will naturally judge all other people harshly and falsely as well. We act as though we expect perfection from others, when in fact, we are disappointed in our own imperfections. Within this feeling of unworthiness, we will express our fear and negativity outwardly against other people. On this lower energy level we desire to elevate ourselves at the expense of others. Again, this is weakness disguised as strength.

Self-judgment is our way of wanting to be better, but we it leads us down the wrong road to get there. The truth is that our ego-based standards are impossible to attain and do not

151

lead to happiness. This is because we are seeking to experience Divine qualities while functioning within our lower identity, and we are only "good enough" when we feel superior to others.

To get onto the right path, the enlightened path, we first and foremost need an awakening to our higher identity. It is this connection to our Authentic Self that offers access to the love, peace, joy, abundance, wellness, and fulfillment we seek. And you will only find this within yourself, not out in the world.

Most people believe that the expression of love, care, or compassion for others is a mental decision followed by an external action. In other words, your ego has decided for this particular instant or person that it will be generous, and consider someone else's needs. This is not a terrible thing. It is simply limited and unsustainable. The true shift that must occur involves realizing your Authentic Self and endeavoring to heal and grow from within. Your true higher nature is authentically loving, compassionate, and generous.

Once you have awakened to focus on your own inner healing and the development of your inner love, your outer expressions will be supportive to all others seeking to experience their true loving life. As we begin to invest our attention and intention into our true higher self, we will then express our loving qualities to all others as a natural occurrence of living our truth. We are now embracing Unity Consciousness, which is a form of Mastery.

While we each share the adventure of living this human experience, how this actually plays out is necessarily different according to our unique Soul's design. The evolution of our individual Soul varies from person to person, therefore our requirements are not identical. However, the key point for each of us is to honor our true path, and recognize each other's path as equally valid and valuable as our own.

We come into this world from Divine love, and then we learn about fear. We learn to fear our eventual death, even though our spirit knows that we have each lived and died as humans many times before. And it knows that this "death" is merely a transitional event for us.

We learn about physical and emotional pain, and gradually take every precaution to avoid being vulnerable. All the while our spirit knows that it is in overcoming our vulnerabilities that true growth and ascension takes place.

We learn to fear the things that we do not understand or cannot control. So we identify and attach to that which is familiar to us, and judge all else as inferior, foolish, immoral, or evil. Obviously then, people who look or think "that way," or who come from "that place," are a threat to us and our ideals. In order to protect ourselves and our determination of "truth," we decide that we must either convert them or destroy them.

Inhabiting the principles of Unity and Equality does not mean that our life paths require the same conditions and circumstances in human terms. It means that even with all of our human differences and varying life paths, we are each worthy, valuable, and deserving of the same opportunity for Divine fulfillment. We all have the right to life, love, peace, wellness, freedom, and the pursuit of happiness. And in an energy that does not directly harm another, we get to choose how best to achieve and experience these qualities.

Is it the will of the Divine that all people have equal financial wealth, health, loving relationships, etc.? No, these are human qualities that need to be addressed by each person within their human experience. Varying amounts of effort, skill, and training, in the application of a vast array of gifts, qualities, and passions, will certainly dictate countless degrees of human success. Again, we chose different paths and conditions for very specific reasons of personal growth, healing, and transformation.

Therefore, these different paths will obviously generate different lifestyle results. It is only our ego that determines love, peace, wellness, freedom, and the pursuit of happiness as coming from our external human conditions. To Spirit, each of these positive qualities are available within the range of circumstance and experience of any life path, because they are internally generated.

Following this logic, regardless of the appearance of our life, we are to have an equal opportunity to express and experience the Divine qualities and to fulfill our Soul's higher purpose. Yet, Unity suggests that our individual Soul purpose and life path was designed to interconnect with that of other Souls (humans). Therefore, for the sake of our own growth, healing, and ascension, our highest expression is to support other people on their path. However, just as our ego judge's value and success in human terms, it is within this ego energy that we will seek an advantage over others, to their detriment.

We all ask for compassion, mercy, justice, kindness, and human rights for ourselves. Yet, while attached to ego, we too easily turn a blind eye to other humans asking for the same thing. We too often do everything we can to not notice their suffering. We think that it is not our job or purpose to assist or share with others. We tell our kids to share their toys, yet as adults we will offer death threats to anyone who suggests we share our resources.

Equality stipulates that all people are afforded the same rights. And that no one, based upon their human circumstances, should be held above or below any other human. Any person or society that routinely promotes inequality is not living or functioning in an enlightened manner, and is therefore, in need of awakening.

Does it make sense to anyone else that maybe those who designed easier human paths included as part of their evolution the objective of ascending to the loving qualities of generosity and compassion? And therefore, a large part of their fulfillment will come in offering kindness, service, and assistance to the Souls that chose a harsher physical reality. If this is true, are you willing to fulfill your Soul's purpose in this life? This is not just about those with relative financial wealth, though it logically would start there. However, each of us has an opportunity to focus more on loving service.

And, maybe the people who exhibit greater human need, on a Soul level, aspired to experience the loving qualities of humility and gratitude. Therefore, they have created the conditions to allow others to help them. Within the awareness of enlightened living each of these individuals is benefiting on both a soul and human level. This is Unity Consciousness.

Within the existing ego-state of human functioning neither individual is truly fulfilled. One is too attached to their identity as advantaged/entitled, and their fear of lack won't allow them to share their possessions or skills. And the other is too caught up in victim mentality to ask for help or maximize their own contribution within their range of opportunity.

If the well-off person thinks the person in need is basically lazy, worthless, and a burden on society, he is living in fear and is not expressing loving energy. This does not support the advancement of the Soul or the elevation of the collective consciousness on Earth. If the disadvantaged person was to live in the fearful energy of resentment, distrust, hopelessness, and victimhood, he would not achieve his Soul's purpose. And he would neither elevate his consciousness nor be empowered to improve his human condition.

Is the design of our human path always an easy explanation in all cases according to our human understanding? No. There are people all over the world who seemingly exist in deplorable conditions. Some of these are due to a lack of resources and others to maniacal tyranny. As I have said, there are many levels of consciousness exhibited by humans in this world. Whether through karmic balancing or some other explanation beyond our reasoning mind, seemingly innocent people are being subjected to inhumane circumstances.

It is not my intention to ignore or otherwise explain this away. It is my goal to emphasize that which each of us can do to elevate our own level of consciousness. We can heal within and serve to the best of our ability within the context of our life path. What higher purpose does it serve to abandon any idea of personal accountability, growth, and healing, because of a lack of understanding about someone else's spiritual/human journey?

Individually we may not be able to overthrow a dictator or provide food and medicine to impoverished people, yet, we still have a responsibility to love them (and ourselves). As we awaken in our own life we will desist in adding our fearful energy into the world, and begin to shift the tide by expanding the reach of our loving energy. If we simply stand back in judgment, whether we express fear, hate, or sadness, we are adding to the darkness. If you can help someone directly, please do so. If not, recognize the light of their truth, and honor them with loving energy.

Promoting Unity and equality starts as an inside job. More of us need to take responsibility for our own awakening and enlightened living. Be accountable for the positive things that you can do in your life. See the need for your light in the world, and then focus your more powerful love energy in this direction.

Everyone has the right and the responsibility to connect with and honor their own path of Divinity, without judgment and condemnation, as long as their path is not directly dangerous to others. However, the laws that govern a land should be both free from bias and tolerant of all traditions in order to support equality. For whatever differences we have chosen in our human experience, the opportunities for growth and happiness must be available to all. They must not be restricted arbitrarily by the power brokers who are merely acting for their own gain and the proliferation of their disempowering point of view.

As a human society we need more people to heal and evolve in order to elevate the consciousness on the planet. As we are able to do this we will develop the human rights and welfare policies to support those in need. We all need to evolve and share our light as we rise up to be part of the solution.

CHAPTER 21

The Energy of Fear Promoted
in the World

*"Love is what we were born with.
Fear is what we learned here."*

- Marianne Williamson

Many people think that they are informed responsible world citizens by ritualistically following the news each day. You may tune in to one of the numerous news stations on television, read a local or national newspaper, or get your news from the internet or social media. Regardless of how accurate you may think this information is, your energy is being impacted, and the way you perceive your world is likely being corrupted.

Since nearly all of what is reported promotes fear, you are constantly being conditioned within this negative energy. Not unexpectedly, most people who are so attached to the "news" are filled with fear and judgment. Plus, you may be spending hours per day that could be otherwise more productive for developing or sharing loving energy. Additionally, for those who consume this negativity just prior to going to sleep, you are feeding this toxicity to your mind which now must ruminate this fear for the next several hours.

Most of the news reported by humans is biased and not objective. As far as that is concerned, most of the history we have learned is not objective either. Every story is told from someone's perspective. And those in power and control tend to dictate the message that promotes their ego perception. Be careful not to blindly attach your allegiance to someone else's point of view. Always endeavor to connect your energy to the things that bring/share your higher truth and value.

The media is much like the bookmakers in Las Vegas. There is action (viewership/ratings) on both sides of the competition (political/social/ideological issues). And the media moguls make loads of money either way. Those who are most divisive will garner the most attention and coverage. Typically they are directly promoting great fear and judgment, and not Unity and equality. Their only real message is that someone (or group) is trying to take away something essential to you. They are stirring up the energy of fear within their group or base. This is not solution oriented, and it is very disempowering.

I am not suggesting that you be uniformed about what is going on in your neighborhood or in the world. However, I am recommending that your primary focus should always be to monitor your energy and endeavor to abide in love. This will require you to use higher awareness in order to balance your viewing and investing in the information being broadcast. Most everyone has an agenda that is intended to sway or sell you.

When it comes to the reporting of our worldly events, the consequence (intended or not) may be the corruption of your energy. And this is detrimental to your holistic wellness. What this really means is that the energy of fear that already exists on a toxic level within you is being reinforced in a continual and powerful way.

And just as ego stands for Edging God Out, this fear is pushing aside your identity with your Authentic Self and your loving energy. You hear things that eventually attach to your specific brand of self-interest, and now you are negatively charged against someone (or some group) in the world. You likely will never be directly affected by this person/cause, yet through your energy, the impact is accumulative and devastating toward creating your false reality.

Today our news reports the tragedies, crimes against humanity, and corrupt systems, companies, or groups that are judged unethical or dangerous. Much of this comes from the perspective of judging someone as right or wrong depending upon the point of view of the reporting source. So, what gets reported, and what goes unreported? Who is making these choices and why?

Many national stories simply display the worst possible actions and behaviors that mankind is capable of committing upon their fellow man. How often do we hear about the good, kind, and loving acts? You can see why the development of Unity and equality must come from within, from our higher nature.

I am encouraging responsible viewing or non-attachment to the worst of humanity. Every day (24/7) there is some "Breaking News" about the latest tragedy, or some ridiculous statement or action from a high profile person. Then nothing is resolved, and we just move on to the next day's drama. We get no solutions, only continuous broadcasting, and the endless debate of biased pros and cons.

Yes, these events are occurring somewhere on the planet and there are some very dangerous and unconscious people in the world. However, it is the constant bombardment of negativity that renders the masses incapacitated by anger and hopelessness - FEAR. We personalize this energy which is disempowering, and then we share it with others in order to connect in our misery. Viewing the suffering of others has become a disturbing form of entertainment for many people. This is an unenlightened path.

Instead of instantly attaching to the information from the media as infallible truth, filter this through the lens of love and Unity Consciousness. Don't be the well-trained rodent who proudly accepts the poisonous pellet and thinks he is nourished. Be courageous and disciplined enough to set your own standards for the information and input you receive daily.

Wherever possible, use the information reported as a way to get involved and help heal and eradicate injustice where you can. Live in your highest power, send love and light to wherever it is needed, and seek to take the actions you can take to help someone in need. Simply attaching your energy to the suffering of others is disempowering for you and unsupportive of them.

Ask yourself some important questions, "Is this objectively informative or is someone feeding me their bias?" And, more importantly, "Does this information inspire me to be more loving and compassionate, or does it lead me to judge someone or something through fear?" And, "Is this news supportive to my well-being or at least informative without disempowering me?" Use your awareness to shine the light of higher truth upon the energy that you take in. Once again, enlightenment is about accountability.

Sometimes people act as if desecrating or maligning the character of another person or group is humorous. But in truth this comes from deep-seated fear and even self-hatred. You see this often in a political, racial, national, or religious context. Beyond a mere disagreement in policy or perspective, there is great comradery in the consumption of a shared negativity. In very disappointing ways, social media has exacerbated this problem.

We have de-evolved into the unconscious expression of negative and harmful energy, and far too many people are fully ego-identified. It is critical that as individuals we begin to nurture Self-Mastery or Self-Realization. This is critical if we are to recover and evolve, we must align and connect with the energy of love that is a shared higher identity and the responsibility of all humans/Souls.

CHAPTER 22
Waking Up from Fear

"As we are liberated from our own fear, our presence automatically liberates others."

- Marianne Williamson

Day by day we get sucked into this vortex of fear-based negative energy. It's no wonder so many people feel angry, hopeless, and powerless in their lives. We have grown so weary and complacent about the sheer volume of death, destruction, inequality, and injustice, that we are numb to the cause and oblivious to the remedy.

As people are dying or suffering in horrific ways, we should be noticing that our present way of living is unsupportive to our individual and collective well-being. But instead, we just feel relief when it does not directly affect us or those close to us. And we retreat further into our fear and mistrust of our fellow humans.

The real truth is that many Souls are sacrificing their human experience in order to awaken humanity to the real root of the problem. We are stuck in an ego-based delusion, and these highly-evolved Beings are choosing to design their human experience in a way that draws attention to the world's needless suffering and violence. They may be children or other innocents who came to teach us truth. Yet we are too self-involved to notice.

We need to Wake Up! Our focus must shift to Unity Consciousness and loving energy, and away from constant fear and blame. We feel sadness for the victims and hopelessness for humanity. In this way we keep our distance and avoid responsibility for making the necessary changes within ourselves. And often we feel justified in our hateful and angry views toward the perpetrators, even though we know (or care) nothing about their life challenges and disadvantages. None of this fearful energy will solve anything

We have many people who are sick and unconscious (unaware of their higher truth) and we are not providing the assistance they need. Until we begin to awaken to the real truth that, as a society, we are no better than the most challenged and disadvantaged of us, we will continue to be "shocked and appalled," while healing and fixing nothing. The principles of Unity and equality promote the practical application of our loving energy toward the issues of physical/mental/spiritual wellness.

We must begin to release our fear and elevate our consciousness, which supports our own healing and connection to love. In doing this, we may apply our great creativity, intentions, and resources toward real solutions based in love. Otherwise we will continue to support separateness, and will build up the weaponry to fight fear with fear.

Self-Mastery is the approach and process for transformation. Even as one who endeavors to walk an enlightened path, we will occasionally have our own fear and doubt arise from within. This is due to the residue of fear-based energy from a lifetime of negative conditioning.

When this appears to my awareness, I take and recommend the following steps. One, don't panic. Each present moment is temporary, and the next one may bring a new higher energy. Two, with your awareness, shift to the offense (sports term). In other words, instead of defending or dwelling in your fearful energy, fill your mind with positive self-talk, affirmations, and gratitude. Drown out the fear and doubt with the energy that reflects your higher truth. And three, allow and accept this new energy with peace, patience, and understanding. Resist the "need" to instantly solve or fix the perceived mental problem your ego has conjured up.

Humans have fear in their heart that leads them to many delusions and harmful actions. The first way in which we each can begin to promote Unity is to stop condemning groups of people who are simply associated in ways that are beyond our own experience or understanding. Stop hurling jokes and insults that are venomous with the poison of hate and intolerance.

Again, I am sometimes disheartened to see the fear and hate so casually expressed in a meme or posting on social media. As part of your development, please do not encourage those who still express this fear. They are ignorant of their higher truth – and now you are not.

As far as religion goes, many people are moving away from the established ways because they have not effectively changed or evolved with the times. I would love to promote that we honor the various religious traditions which have great meaning to the people involved. My only request would be to eliminate the fear and hate expressed in our religions. It all too often promotes judgment from a place of intolerance and false authority, condemning the ideas and paths that are different than its own teaching.

The greatest examples of love, tolerance, peace, and unity should be promoted within our spiritual institutions. After all, the Master in whom the religion was founded invariably taught these principles. I believe that the movement toward more people claiming to be spiritual, as opposed to religious, will ultimately shift some of the outdated and discriminatory views within the religions. We can only evolve, or be destroyed; there is no staying the same or going back. Waking up from fear is a higher purpose that we all share, and is our key to enlightened living.

CHAPTER 23
Elevating Consciousness

"When we grow in our consciousness, there will be more compassion and more love, and then the barriers between people, between religions, between nations will begin to fall. Yes, we have to beat down separateness."

- Ram Dass

When we express the inner light of love onto our own path, we are simultaneously adding our light into the world. Our light serves to enlighten others as well. As more of us are focused on living in this way, we cause the collective consciousness to shift toward love and light. This may seem unfathomable to the ego mind, due to the sheer quantity of humans presently living in fear. Yet this is how energy works. Loving energy is expansive, and it is aligned with the true higher nature of all humans/Souls.

Embracing Unity Consciousness offers the highest form of love for humanity, individually and collectively. Its truest expression is to treat others as we would want to be treated. These are more than mere words which sound good in theory; this must be the goal of each and every enlightened human. And those of us on this path must continue to heal, grow, and ascend to a place of practicing this edict in all we do.

As far off as this way of human involvement may seem, it is in fact in alignment with our true highest nature – our Authentic Self. The process of mastering our lives begins with our recognition of this empowering truth (Part I). Next, we develop a greater more consistent connection to this higher nature by practicing mindfulness and choosing to express loving energy in each present moment (Part II). And finally, we have elevated our consciousness, and we have shifted our perception of ourselves, and therefore all others. We now know that we are each Divine Beings simply on our own unique paths in this human experience (Part III).

As we are able to grow and evolve in our enlightenment we will seek out more opportunities to offer and promote love, peace, kindness, compassion, and joy in service to each other. Together we could be utilizing this human experience to support all life. In doing this we would create opportunities for greater contribution from all people who embrace their higher nature and offer their greatest gifts, passions, and purpose to the world. We could literally meet all of our human needs should we decide to increase our level of consciousness and awaken to our higher truth. No one should be hungry, homeless, or die from easily-curable diseases.

I realize that to many this sounds crazy, naïve, and even blasphemous. Accordingly, we have held to the ego-based system of power, control, and "every person for themselves." It is true, of course, that life can continue for a time in this less evolved and disempowering paradigm.

However, without awakening and evolving to Unity Consciousness, we are on a track of diminished resources and uninhabitable conditions on our planet. We will continue to see more of our population unable to adequately care for themselves or contribute to the welfare of society. Therefore, many of those who think themselves "successful" will be required to support the rest, or be overthrown.

The voices of the oppressed will continue to speak out, and if not heard, their actions will surely be noticed. In this way, the collective consciousness works the same as our own individual consciousness. We have an inner voice of truth (intuition), which, if we listen, will guide us to our higher path of evolution without the necessity of extraordinarily challenging experiences. In other words we advance without unnecessarily creating our own suffering. Now, having lived so connected to our self-interest and fear, humanity is on a path of great suffering. The key, as always, is awakening.

The greatest threat to our peace and happiness is to continue to ignore the plight of those who are greatly disadvantaged in our society. We have pitted race against race, nationality against nationality, religion against religion, and gender against gender. This is short-sighted and very disempowering for all involved. For us as humans to continue to be mired in self-interest, with little or no compassion for others in need is a very low threshold of consciousness, and far less than we are capable of and designed to be. Something has to give; as they say, "pay me now or pay me later."

We cannot just say that this doomsday scenario will likely "not happen in our lifetime, so don't bother me with this stuff, I am doing fine." Instead, this is where we need a new education in wisdom. And we need more people living enlightened, because our opportunity is now, while we are still participating in our human experience here on Earth. It's time to begin, through our own accountability, to shift the energy of the collective consciousness toward a greater awareness of our power to make a positive difference for all.

We must be committed to our focus on inner healing and expressions of love in each present moment. And at the same time, we must release our attachment to the fear promoted in the world. Refrain from joining into the negativity all around you, this is discouraging and disempowering. Apply self-discipline in your process of self-mastery. And be content within your energy and effort, without needing to control others. Otherwise, this is where ego tarnishes a spiritual endeavor.

Although the consequences of not elevating our consciousness will likely be dire, this is not a choice for transformation out of fear. It is fear that has put us on this path of clear and present danger, and it is love that is the antidote. Awakening and evolving comes from your higher connection to love. Hearts and minds must open to the reality that all people are truly alike on a level beyond the differences in their appearance and beliefs. And then new opportunities will be created for all of us to flourish in this world.

I do not share this as if this is a quick and easy transformation, where the majority of humans will suddenly awaken. The truth is that we are each here on our own personal journey of evolution and service, and we must each decide our identity for ourselves. Not all beings are functioning within their human experience at the same level of consciousness. Some minds are still ignorant of the higher possibilities, while others are controlled by an ego that defies the very idea of enlightened living.

Therefore, those who are open and ready to shift toward Unity Consciousness must lead the way. This takes incredible courage to forge the higher path through the army of resistance and fear. Yet, for the sake of your highest wellbeing this is the greatest path.

You may now awaken and begin to heal, grow, and evolve, step by step. As you develop this love within, find ways to connect with others from the space of loving energy. It is fine to start with those closest to you, as they certainly need your loving expressions. However, learn to step outside of your comfort zone and show kindness and compassion toward someone in need, whom you have not previously met. This is quite fulfilling and imminently useful.

Open to the idea of Unity Consciousness as a goal for creating your new perspective on reality. With increased awareness of the present moment, catch yourself when you judge or condemn another person (or yourself), and then intentionally shift your thoughts to a more loving expression.

Five Limitless Thoughts – Developing Bodhisattva Heart

I would like to share these 5 powerful prayers from the Buddhist tradition, as they relate perfectly with the mindset of Unity Consciousness. Notice how these are supportive of positive, healthy human conditions for all. Buddhists consider this far more valuable than wealth and power.

May all living beings have happiness and its causes.

May all be free from unhappiness and its causes.

May all dwell in equanimity, free from attraction and aversion.

*May all quickly attain the great happiness
which lies beyond all misery.*

May all enjoy inner and outer peace, now and forever.

CHAPTER 24

Oneness is the End of Duality

"All differences in this world are of degree, and not of kind, because oneness is the secret of everything."

- Swami Vivekananda

On the path of enlightenment there are always levels beyond levels, peaks to climb and valleys to transcend. In this book I have focused on three significant steps to assist you in transforming to greater self-mastery in your life. In teaching this wisdom I have spent much time comparing the energy of Spirit to ego.

These two energies/identities, one aligned with love and the other with fear, have come to define our engagement and potential within our life path. I have used these terms as illustration of enlightenment versus delusion, peace versus suffering, wellness versus pain, acceptance versus judgement, etc. This wisdom represents a great variance in the way we have come (chosen) to experience our human life. Are we going to integrate our Spirit into our humanity, or are we going deny our Spirit at the expense of our highest fulfillment and connection to love?

The higher truth is that all things are made up of the one Divine energy.

Accordingly, the higher levels of consciousness recognize only Oneness. However, as humans, in need of awakening, we have chosen to experience our humanity from the perspective of duality. Therefore, I have elected to utilize these principals in my teaching.

The existence of duality in humans causes our minds to focus on separation, fear, and judgment, and this then becomes our reality. We actually feel more comfortable with the idea that there is good versus evil, right or wrong, us against them. This is how we have chosen to perceive ourselves and the world around us. And this has created a world fraught with all manner of delusion, competition, and conflict.

Our misconception has even taught that God or Divinity has a duplicitous nature. That "She" loves some even while afflicting others, or "He" rewards some with "heaven," while condemning others to an eternity in a burning "hell." Yet in truth, Universal Intelligence (Divine Energy, Source, God, or whatever name you prefer) consists ONLY in the energy and nature of love.

We are not judged and condemned for our failures or missteps. Instead, these simply lead to consequences that impact our human experience in a challenging way. Even so, we always have the opportunity to heal, grow, and ascend during our human life. And this speaks to the significance of personal accountability connected to higher truth.

Source only has compassion and unconditional love for us – as we are part of it. This is Oneness. Within our human experience we are simply working to find our higher truth and evolve according to our Soul's needs and purpose. I do not have a full explanation that may satisfy all of your queries, nor is that my job or purpose.

Yet, I do feel comfortable in teaching empowerment based upon free will, our true higher identity, and the complete loving benevolence of Source. Interesting how our worship of duality has created our perception of God. On the one hand, man fears God and claims to be unworthy sinners. While on the other hand, men have freely defined God to be as limited and fear-based as them. Aside from the delusion factor, you can see from history how this has worked out, with different groups of men determining that only THEIR views and definitions must be followed and honored by all. Otherwise, God will be upset and offended. In all ways our ego-nature deflects and obscures our realization of truth – to our own detriment.

Instead, like Source, our essence is energy created in love. We are not good or evil, right or wrong, saved or condemned, light or dark, etc. Even while our thoughts and actions will at times be harmful or negative, it does not define our true higher identity and potential. Our experiences may feel good or bad to us, but they are simply a device that impacts us and others according to our need to balance or realign our energy with truth.

Are we connected to love in this moment or are we temporarily disconnected? As we are able to notice our energy we may consciously choose to shift toward more loving expressions. That's it – no judgment, fear, false identification, or attachment, just the results of the movement of energy.

This may not yet fully resonate as truth for you. Yet, I decided to share this as a peek into your potential as an enlightened spiritual being having a human experience. Our perspective of Oneness over duality authorizes us to fully embrace our own Divinity, as well as Unity Consciousness.

In truth, heaven or hell is right here with us now – determined according to our level of consciousness. In Heaven – you unconditionally love yourself and others. In Hell – you fear and judge yourself and others. At times we will each live within either place or energy.

With greater awareness and accountability you can choose to express and experience the energy of love – your higher nature. Otherwise, you may continue to reside in your lower ego identity and experience life as you have. The beauty is that you have free will to determine how you will live your life. No judgement, only consequences. You are on a spiritual journey that supports you in the ways that you need for healing, growth, and ascension. However, your time table is of your own choosing.

We will surely continue to have experiences that offer us challenges, and opportunities for further healing and growth. But now, with the wisdom you have been taught, you can choose to recognize this as beneficial to your evolution. Otherwise, with the old teaching, you will easily get caught up in your delusion of fear (blame, judgment, anger, resentment, disappointment, hopelessness, anxiety, etc.), and continue to create suffering.

You are here on the Earth plane to learn and practice to be more of what you truly are - a Divine Being. This is your spiritual practice and evolution. And it must be integrated moment by moment into the details of your human experiences and life. Sometimes you fall short (disconnect) and make a mistake or disempowering choice. Love YOURSELF anyway. And at times someone else falls short of their highest nature and makes choices that seem to impact you negatively. Love THEM anyway. This is enlightened living and Unity Consciousness.

CHAPTER 25

The Path of an Awakened Master

"Ignoring all prejudices of caste, creed, class, color, sex, or race, a swami follows the precepts of human brotherhood. His goal is absolute unity with spirit."

- Paramahansa Yogananda

From wherever you are at this time - physically/ spiritually/ mentally/ emotionally - you have an opportunity to begin to awaken to a higher truth about yourself. There are always practical steps you can take to shift your awareness on the path of healing, growth, and ascension of consciousness. You can redefine yourself by accepting that your higher nature is Divine Spirit. This opens the space for opportunities that do not exist when you are only identifying with your human/ego challenges and unsatisfactory experiences.

Next, you can develop a practice of present-moment mindfulness and awareness that supports you in making the most empowering choices for your own well-being. You can be more aware of when you are stuck in the disempowering thoughts that have led you to negative consequences and harmful relationships. You can practice connecting to your space of love (the quality of Spirit) which reinforces your power to maintain positive thoughts, words, and actions in each present moment.

Now you are accountable and more in tune with defining the steps you can take that are a progression to greater truth and fulfillment in your life. Your happiness does not depend on the endless desperate seeking for the things or conditions that you don't have, but think you should. There is much greater value in living your higher truth and creating the conditions that are most supportive to your unique path of wellness. There is no enlightenment without accountability. Therefore, do the inner work and find the gratitude for all that you do have and for the progress you are making.

Finally, to be awakened and enlightened requires that we not only realize our own higher truth for healing, growth, and evolution, but that we support all others in their process as well. You are Divine Spirit, they are Divine Spirit, and no one is greater or lesser. You are on your unique spiritual journey within this human experience, and the same is true for all others. Their path will look different than yours, but regardless, it is equally powerful and valuable.

When you find and live the true light of love within, you will wish this for all others as well. And where possible, you will support and assist other people, to alleviate their suffering. Notice when you find judgment of or separation from another. This is a sign TO YOU that you are connected to fear and not living your higher truth. If it is your intention to awaken to enlightened living, you may use your awareness to recognize this attachment to ego, and choose to heal and shift to love.

The power is yours to use or to ignore. Free will ensures that we always have a choice. And our experiences always reflect our choices. All things are energy and we can either express love or fear. How accountable are you willing to be toward elevating the quality of the experiences and life that you are creating? And, how do you want your energy to impact the world? My hope is that you will choose the Enlightened Path and become an Awakened Master.

"I bow to that Divine Light within all Beings" - Namaste

PART III: Exercises

1) Take some time to focus inwardly to notice your present beliefs. How do you view or value those who may never directly benefit you (Ex. other than family, friends, co-workers, etc.)? Can you notice the inner fear that has caused you to perceive others as a threat?

2) If after doing Exercise #1, you determine that you have any bias or negative judgments against any person or group of people, examine this further. How real are these grievances to you today? Do you see that this negativity is hindering your own wellness and darkening your own path? Consider deeply the steps you may take to heal and shift your views to be in alignment with Unity Consciousness?

3) Determine something that you can do in the next 30 days as a way to offer kindness, compassion, and support to someone less advantaged than you. Using your developing connection to enlightenment, endeavor to do this in some form or other on a regular or consistent basis.

PART III: Affirmations

I AM elevating my consciousness – always and in all ways.

I AM grateful for the love, peace, and joy in the world.

I AM offering love and light to all Beings.

I AM living in the Light.

I AM connected to the Oneness of all Life.

I AM empowered to make a positive difference in the world.

I AM a Divine Being.

I AM Embracing Unity Consciousness.

I AM Loved and Honored by All.

I AM a loving and compassionate Being.

I AM an Awakened Master, how may I serve?

ABOUT THE AUTHOR

Scott E. Clark brings his own practical life experience into his writing. He has learned valuable life lessons leading to his own ongoing transformational development. Some of his roles, titles, relationships, and responsibilities, include son, father, grandfather, husband, friend, employee, business owner, student, teacher, mentor, and author.

His highest intention for his writing and teaching is to offer a philosophy and path that may guide others to recognize their true potential through personal accountability and higher identity. This is attained through inner healing and growth, and then expressed out into the world. Even while spending 30 years in business, primarily in accounting management, his passion introduced him to the higher principles and possibilities of life.

His foundation in spiritual understanding is to include and accept all people as equal spiritual beings who are each on their own unique path of consciousness and evolution. It is from this perspective and energy that he has written, *"On the Enlightened Path,"* as the inspired message he has been guided to share. His natural inclination toward balance, logic, and practicality, serves his purpose of introducing the integration of spiritual principles into everyday life.

Current and future books in the *"On the Enlightened Path"* series will address the topics of: Self-Mastery, Relationships, Career, Health, Parenting, and more.

Mr. Clark recognizes that there are many road maps to higher wisdom and inspiration, and for each of us it is a matter of finding our own path of truth. Some examples of the various ancient and contemporary books and wisdom teachings that have inspired him on his journey are: *Buddhism, A Course in*

Miracles, Kriya Yoga, Tao Te Ching, The Bhagavad Gita, The Yoga Sutras, The Power of Now, The Four Agreements, The Law of Attraction, and many more.

Mr. Clark is also the author of, "The Empower Model for Men: a guide to more conscious living," published in 2014. After his extensive professional business career, as an accounting and financial manager and CPA, he now serves as an author, teacher, and mentor in the field of personal and spiritual growth and wellness. Aside from this "significant" career change in his fifties, Mr. Clark engages in a daily meditation practice and fitness routine. As he continues to fulfill his higher purpose in service to the world, he cherishes time with his children, grandchildren, family, and friends.

www.ingramcontent.com/pod-product-compliance
Lightning Source LLC
Chambersburg PA
CBHW071218090426
42736CB00014B/2873